CH?RCH

W9-BBS-060

THE JOHANNINE COUNCIL

THE JOHANNINE COUNCIL

Witness to Unity

BERNARD HÄRING

Translated by Edwin G. Kaiser

HERDER AND HERDER

1963
HERDER AND HERDER   NEW YORK
232 Madison Avenue, New York 16, N.Y.

First edition 1963
Second impression 1964

Original edition "Konzil im Zeichen der Einheit,"
Verlag Herder K.G., Freiburg im Breisgau, 1963.

Imprimi potest: John J. Byrne, C.PP.S.
                  Provincial

Nihil obstat: Leonard J. Kostka, C.PP.S.
                  Censor deputatus

Imprimatur: † John J. Carberry
                  Bishop of Lafayette in Indiana
                  April 9, 1963

Library of Congress Catalog Card Number: 63–18151
© 1963, Herder and Herder, Incorporated
Printed in the United States of America

CONTENTS

FOREWORD

In varying degrees, it can be said that the whole world is aware that we are entering a new and glorious era in the history of the Church. Enthusiasm generated by this awareness is similar to the joy of the just and devout Simeon who lived out his days in expectation of the consolation of Israel.

The Pontificate of Pope John XXIII and the Second Vatican Council are signs and generators of this new age which, it is hoped, will witness a flowering of the charity, justice and unity of the Gospel. The distinguished author of *The Johannine Council: Witness to Unity* has beautifully yet succinctly explained the Council in this perspective.

Appropriately, Father Bernard Häring introduces his work with an exposition of the Johannine theme of the Council. He reminds us that from the time of his proclamation of the Council, Pope John placed it under the protection of St. John the Baptist and St. John the Evangelist. We cannot escape the reflection that the reign of Pope John XXIII imitated the spirit of these great Saints. Like the Precursor, the Holy Father labored steadfastly to "make straight the way of the Lord". After the fashion of the Evangelist, he taught his "little children" by his example to love one another and became for us all the Beloved Apostle.

It is my prayer that each reader of this volume will be inspired to bring to fruition the Johannine Era of the Church.

JOSEPH CARDINAL RITTER
Archbishop of St. Louis

TRANSLATOR'S PROLOGUE

In its free and open discussion the Second Vatican Council reflected the generous spirit of John XXIII. Though the Pope's authority, defined by the First Vatican, is clear and uncontested, his guidance—by contrast with that of Pius IX and the previous Council—was largely by example and suggestion. Following the lead of the Holy Father, the Council is now clearly moving in the direction of a tremendous pastoral goal, adapting its course boldly to modern needs with little stress on condemnations of error or explicit definitions of revealed truth. The contrast with Trent and First Vatican is actually startling, and can be explained only by the difference in the Church's relation to the world in our time. In the past the Church has abstained from formal definition or defined her doctrine in the most circumspect terms for weighty pastoral reasons, but this is the first Council in history in which the official position has been to avoid specific dogmatization and specific condemnation. Now the Church in council assembled proclaims anew her service to Christ in the spirit of unity and love, in response to Christ's own prayer that all may be one.

Conciliar literature is already abundant; every theme has been touched upon, statistics, economics, politics, the liturgy. The present work by the distinguished author of *The Law of Christ* is unique in its penetration to the very heart of the mystery of the Church, viewed in her response to the Master: the whole Church is seen to respond to the *kairos*, the hour of grace. Here we have the approach of the pastoral theologian. Some Catholics wanted a curial council as they favor a curial government of the Church; some stressed the legal institutional aspects of the Church even in relation to the Council; some looked to condemnations of error as a principal task, coupled with a stress on further dogmatic decrees. But, as Father Häring shows, the Council has followed the thought of John XXIII in stressing an essentially pastoral plan and design. Though many of the observations in this book seem bold, the more the author departs from commonplace views, the more deeply he is rooted in the most venerable traditions of the apostolic Church. The book is orientated, as is the Council, toward the Johannine theme.

In choosing the name John after his election, the pope begged God that the voices of John the Baptist and John the Evangelist, calling for penance and loving unity, might be heard in the whole Church through "our humble pastoral office." Our growth in Christ, through the promotion of truth in love, he indicated in another address, is a sure indication of progress. The ideal of the Council and of the Pope of the Council is the Church stripped of all that could in any way make her eternal message less effective. Such is the basic theme of *The Johannine Council: Witness to Unity.* The reader, we are convinced, will find it a fruitful commentary on the current concept of the

Church in her sacramental-sacrificial structure: she is the continuation of Christ's work on earth, the basic sacrament of the Word, the sacred call to service in Christ.

The translator is grateful to the faculty of St. Joseph's Collge for encouragement and assistance, particularly to Fathers Joseph Lazur and Aloysius O'Dell for their careful study of the manuscript, and to Mr. and Mrs. John Groppie for a painstaking stylistic revision. It should be noted that the final text in English, though it faithfully presents the thought of Father Häring, does not rigidly adhere to the original German, but reflects in some details the Italian version which was supervised by the author himself.

EDWIN G. KAISER, C.PP.S.
St. Joseph's College
Rensselaer, Indiana

Introduction

The Johannine Theme
of the Second Vatican Council

From the first moment of its proclamation, the Second Vatican Council was placed under the sign and symbol of the mystery of unity by John XXIII; under the sign of John the Baptist, the great preacher of conversion from sin, who signifies the return of all men to the paternal heart of God; and under the sign of the beloved disciple John the Evangelist, who explained the meaning of conversion in all its depth as participation in the mystery of love of God in fraternal love. Accordingly, the Holy Father vigorously underlined the same theme in his address at the opening of the Council on October 11, 1962. He called the fathers' attention to "the great mystery of that unity for which Christ Jesus prayed so ardently to His heavenly Father on the eve of His sacrifice."[1]

Meanwhile, our aspirations have crystallized: we hope that all the prayers, reflections and decisions of the Council will be characterized by this spirit and will develop along

[1] [The Holy Father's address will be found in the Appendix at the end of this book.—Tr.]

these lines. The grand design is apparent, whether we have in mind only the subsequent actions of the Pope or also the discussions in the Vatican Basilica. As we see it at this writing, the Second Vatican Council is the grand Council of the Church endeavoring to grasp her own essence and mission in the light of the "great mystery of unity."

Moved by a desire to live in union with the mind of the Church of the Council, we present the following reflections as an attempt to gain a deeper insight into the unfathomable meaning of this mystery of unity and to grasp its mission in this hour of grace. In this spirit, indeed, we must make the effort to accept the directives of the Council and to put them into action.

The Church of the Second Vatican Council, who examines herself anew regarding her permanent mission and her task for this our time, does not in any exclusive sense turn merely to herself. She finds her task solely in the light of the mystery of the triune love of God, made manifest in Christ Jesus. She examines her conscience and ponders her mission in the light of the "great mystery of unity" to which she must give testimony. In humble prayer she strives for her own deeper conversion to the mystery of unity as she renews her invitation to all Christians to return home; she invites them so that all united will manifest and attest to this mystery and thus cooperate in the redemption of the world.

THE MYSTERY OF UNITY

The world today yearns for unity. The people of the earth are drawn together more closely than ever. For that reason contradictions and divisions make themselves felt all the more painfully. If they are not in some measure made endurable, or if they are not bridged by genuine collaboration among men, they will threaten the whole human race with catastrophe. Men become aware of their solidarity not merely under the pressure of new perils but also in the light of new possibilities, hitherto not imagined but now mutually realizable in the turn of future events.

What can the Church do for the unity of mankind at this turning point in human history? As inevitable as this question may be, it is not basic to the Second Vatican Council. The Council is interested above all in something tremendously more important than mere external unity; she must manifest far more than a simple humanitarian love of all men, for we are one family, the family of God. Indeed, in order to serve the unity of that human family—and for motives still more profound—the Church must reflect, in the light of the supreme mystery, on her unity and on her own witness to unity.

THE REVELATION OF THE MYSTERY OF LOVE
IN THE TRIUNE GOD

The message and the testimony of Christ are in the sign and symbol of the mystery of unity: the very mystery of His substantial union with the Father and in the Holy Spirit. And His mission makes this mystery known to men, sealing it with the testimony of His blood and gathering us into the very orbit of the triune mystery of life and love.

Christ came forth from the Father into the world to render testimony of His substantial union with His Father in essence and in love (see Jn 16,27-28). Salvation of all mankind rests in faith in this mystery. This faith gathers up all men, making them truly one family in God.

The incarnate Son of the eternal Father completes His mission in the power of the Holy Spirit, who is the bond of love between the Son and Father. In the anointing of the Holy Spirit, Christ dedicated Himself totally and utterly to the loving will of the heavenly Father. Thus, in His human nature, in His earthly life, and in His death He reflects His divine mystery, His union with His Father in the Holy Spirit. He is the only-begotten Son, and as the only-begotten Who proceeds from the Father and returns to the Father, He seeks only the glory of the One Who sent Him. In the power of the anointing by the Holy Spirit, the incarnate Son consecrated Himself as expiatory Lamb of sacrifice for the salvation of the whole human race. The Holy Spirit, Personal Love between the Son and Father, moved Him to give witness with a sacrificial love ready for holocaust. This love is at the same time a flame, the flame of sacrifice to the glory of the Father, and the oblation for the salvation of all the brothers and sisters. This sacrificial love gathers up the redeemed of the New Covenant for the banquet of sacrifice, for a testimony of unity and love, ultimately for the festive banquet of eternal life in the light and joy of the triune Love Who is God.

Christ has consecrated His message of the mystery of unity and love with His testimony in His blood. In His blood He has founded the New Covenant. Those who belong to Him share in a new type of blood relationship, completely new, a relationship with Him and through Him with one another. They are made aware of this unity when they grasp the chalice of salvation, invoking together the name of the Lord and thus proclaiming themselves His family. The mystery of the eucharist is a visible and efficacious sign of unity which leads to the ultimate and most tremendous mystery of unity in the bosom of God, one and three.

Jesus came to earth to make the paternal name of God known to us; He is the Father, and because He is Father, He "is love" (I Jn 4,8). God is love in His very essence, giving Himself lovingly, receiving Himself in love, giving again in love in the triune plenitude of the three divine Persons. In Christ Jesus, God, one and three, manifests Himself as love for us, as love which redeems and bestows on us participation in His mystery and His beatitude.

Christ is the Word of the Father unto us, His ultimate and absolute Word, in which He utters all His love. But He is also the Covenant, the response to the Father, the genuine and authentic response of love in the name of all mankind. His sacrifice of expiation for prodigal mankind who deserted the house of the Father is the work of love, a manifestation of the love of the Father. And at the same time it is the sign of the new love present in the heart of creation. In loving obedience and loving zeal for the glory of the Father, Christ manifests the intimate union of His own life with the Father and His incomprehensible solidarity with the human race.

The disciples of Christ partake of the divine Nature through the pure gift of grace. In Him and by means of His blood and through His Spirit, the disciples can give testimony of love like to His and thus remain in Him.

The resurrected Christ sends us the Holy Spirit from the Father. In this Spirit He was baptized. In this Spirit He eagerly accepted the baptism of blood in loving expiation for our salvation and for the glory of the Father. In the same Spirit we cry out together as adopted sons of God and as united brothers, "Abba, Father!" In truth, "The Spirit himself gives testimony to our spirit that we are sons of God" (Rom 8,16).

The name of God is revealed as Father. The name *Father* comes to us through the witness of love. In the love of Jesus

unto death and through the sending of His Spirit Who
unites the redeemed in this love of Christ, God is manifested to us as our Father. Those who together with Christ
recognize the name of God as Father have indeed confessed
through their faith the mystery of the unity between the
Father and the Son: "I have manifested thy name to the
men whom thou hast given me out of the world. . . . Now
they have learnt that whatever thou hast given me is from
thee . . ." (Jn 17, 6-7).

The Mystery of Unity in the Twofold Commandment of Love

Love and unity are not simply a command imposed on
the disciples of Christ. Rather, the mystery embraces them
and, winning their hearts, becomes for them a beatifying
task.

The commandment of love in the Gospel of John calls to
mind the clanging of bells on the Feast of Easter. It is the
sacred refulgence of the mystery of God, of His triune love
shining in splendor on the countenance of Christ. The commandment of the promised land bears no resemblance to the
commandments of the land of slavery. The twofold commandment of love is the manifestation of the mystery—
beatifying and terrifying—of the love of Christ, the love
which turns again to the Father in the sacrifice for the
brethren. "Greater love than this no one has, that one lay
down his life for his friends. You are my friends if you do
the things I command you. No longer do I call you servants,
because the servant does not know what his master does.

But I have called you friends, because all things that I have heard from my Father I have made known to you" (Jn 15,13-15).

The commandment of love given to the disciples is the expression of the commandment which the Father has given to the Son, wherefore it is first a renewed expression of the most intimate communion of life between Father and Son in the Holy Spirit. "As the Father has loved me, I also have loved you. Abide in my love. If you keep my commandments you will abide in my love, as I also have kept my Father's commandments, and abide in his love." (Jn 15,9-10).

What else are the commandments of the eternal Father to the only-begotten Son if not the essential fulfillment of the Son's union of life and love with the Father? He who is given totally as love by the Father gives Himself totally in return with the same love. This giving back overflows into the human nature of Christ united to the divinity; this human nature is the gift of the Father, to be given back to the Father in a sacrificial offering for all men whom the Father has given Him. Because He humbled Himself and lovingly offered Himself in this sacrifice, the Son's human nature is eternally resplendent in the loving majesty of the Father.

For the followers of Christ, all the commandments are summed up in the twofold commandment of love for God and for one's neighbor. Through love for their fellows, which animates everything, they must and can give testimony of the mystery of unity present in them. If they are truly one with Christ, they attest loving obedience for the heavenly Father with fraternal love: "By this will all men know that you are my disciples, if you have love for one another" (Jn 13,35). The community of the followers of Christ—the Church—can give testimony of their love and thus render visible to all the mystery of the love of Christ, precisely because Christ is present in them and because the same mystery of love dwells and works in them through the Holy Spirit—the mystery which Christ has made known and has confirmed with His blood testimony.

The vital union of the disciples with Christ increasingly becomes one with His love and grows in His mystery of union, from which proceeds the love for the Father and the love for the family of men. In the grateful response to Christ's saving love, the disciple unites himself to the love with which Christ returns the love of the eternal Father and with which He offers Himself for those whom the Father has given Him. This truth is clearly expressed in the parting discourse of our Lord at the Last Supper: "If you love me, keep my commandments" (Jn 14,15). My commandments, the Savior says. In this context He means above all both living faith, that joyous acceptance of the saving truth of the mystery of unity and love, and the grateful response of love of God and of one's fellows. The twofold commandment signifies love in union with Christ's love for the heavenly Father and the brethren, a being taken up by the love of the Father as Christ Himself is taken up. In this all the other commandments are contained, and in this alone their fulfillment is assured.

In the discourse at the Last Supper Jesus placed extraordinary emphasis on the mystery character of the command of love. The fulfillment of the double commandment by the disciples is possible solely because the Savior sends them the Spirit of truth, the Spirit of authentic love: "And I will ask the Father and He will give you another Advocate to dwell with you forever, the Spirit of truth . . . . you shall know him, because he will dwell with you, and be in you. . . . you will know that I am in my Father, and you in me, and I in you" (Jn 14,16ff).

The commandment of love, which includes all the other commandments, introduces the community of disciples and every individual disciple constantly and more powerfully, in the measure in which it is fulfilled, into the mystery of the life of the triune love of God: "He who has my commandments and keeps them, he it is who loves me. But he who loves me will be loved by my Father, and I will love him and manifest myself to him." (Jn 14,21).

2

THE CHURCH IN THE MYSTERY OF UNITY

The discourse at the Last Supper leads in a crescendo to
the truth whose climax is in the sacerdotal prayer: that
God's own mystery of love is reflected and revealed to the
world in the loving community of the disciples.

The messianic salvation of which the Savior speaks in
this context is the expression and the effusion of the kingdom of divine love—the fruit of the Holy Spirit (see Jn 14,
24ff). To the degree in which the disciples permit themselves to be guided by the Spirit of Love, that is to the
degree in which they give through fraternal unity the
testimony worthy of faith, the testimony of their loving
union with the Father and the Son, to that degree the joy
and peace of Christ will be perfect in them: "These things
I have spoken to you that my joy may be in you, and that
your joy may be made full" (Jn 15,11).

The words spoken by Jesus in the parting discourse at the
Last Supper, revealing in the new commandment the pressing and emancipating power of the mystery of unity, become still more expressive when we study them in the light
of the eucharist, as the context of John's Gospel plainly

demands. The eucharist is the visible sign, powerful and comprehensible to all the faithful, of fraternal union in the family of God. In the eucharist the Church, festive and ready for sacrifice, celebrates her participation in the paschal mystery of the triumphant love of Christ for the heavenly Father and for all children of men.

Similarly, we must see the sacerdotal prayer as a confident and insistent appeal of the Lord for unity in the community of the disciples, a unity which cannot flow from human prowess or prudence. It is indeed a manifestation of an ineffable mystery. In the eucharist the Church celebrates the Covenant of love with Christ, which ushers her into the supreme mystery of the love and life of God, one and three. The commandment of love committing us to unity is not only the greatest and most pressing precept; it is above all an incomprehensibly great grace, a call to participate in the vocation of Jesus, and like Him, to render the mystery of love in God, one in three, visible and experienceable in faith to the world to give testimony until the end of time to the love of Christ, and through the testimony of unity to proclaim it convincingly to men of good will.

The message and the mission of the Church are not comprehensible if they are divorced from the participation of the disciples in the union of the life of Jesus with the heavenly Father: "I pray for them; not for the world do I pray, but for those whom thou hast given me, because they are thine; and all things that are mine are thine, and thine are mine; and I am glorified in them. . . . I am coming to thee. Holy Father, keep in thy name those whom thou hast given me, that they may be one even as we are" (Jn 17, 9-11).

Consecration of the Church in Truth Through Unity

Christ, the Anointed One, is Himself the truth—the truth of the mystery of the love of God, visibly attested to in Him. The message of the Church is no different. For this the Savior consecrated His own, in the first instance the apostles and their successors, to enable them to bear the message of the truth to men as a flame of love. Only if they participate in His anointing can they be messengers of Christ, witnesses to the mystery of love, which is not a mere supplement to the truth. The truth shines forth in the work of love of Christ. Love is resplendent in the truth, and the truth itself is love, the commitment of love.

The consubstantial Word Whom the Father has sent into the World is at the same time Truth and true testimony of love. "Sanctify them in the truth. Thy word is truth. Even as thou hast sent me into the world, so I also have sent them into the world. And for them I sanctify myself, that they also may be sanctified in truth" (Jn 17, 17-19). Sanctification in truth has in this context substantially the same meaning as the most intimate, powerfully attendant participation in the sacrificial love of Christ, as participation in the vital mystery of unity, and as consecration to the triumphant love which overcomes all egoism and all discord, in which one commits one's life for one's fellow men, and which thus leads men to the feast of the triune love of God.

As Christ confirmed His message—the revelation of the name of the Father as the name of God—by means of His love for men, a love ready to accept death in faithful testimony (Ap 1,5), so love and union among the messengers of the Gospel must bear the witness of faith in the mysteries of salvation to the world. The Gospel, as truth entrusted to the Church, is inseparable from the testimony of love, precisely because it is always and essentially concerned with the truth of the trinitarian love of God, made manifest in the testimony of the love of Christ, and of the Covenant of love between Christ and the Church.

Not only do the apostles penetrate through their faith into the sacred precincts of the great mystery of the divine love revealed in Christ and in the Holy Spirit, but so do all those who through their apostolic word attain to this same faith in this mystery. And thereby, with the apostles, they receive the mission, the consecration, and the charge to give testimony in fraternal unity and love. They must realize that one single word which betrays the unity and love mars the effect of truth. The word which the apostles transmit is both a message of the supreme mystery of unity and an expression of their penetration into that mystery: "Yet not for these only do I pray, but for those also who through their word are to believe in me, that all may be one, even as thou, Father, in me and I in thee; that they also may be one in us, that the world may believe that thou hast sent me" (Jn 17, 20-21).

The word transmitted by the ecclesial community and by fraternal unity is the effect of the majesty of the triune God, turning lovingly toward us and working in us. Participation in the testimony of Christ to the mystery of love is incipient participation in that glory which radiates in the love between Father and Son: "And the glory that thou hast given me, I have given to them, that they may be one, even as we are one: I in them and thou in me; that they may be perfected in unity, and that the world may know that thou hast sent me, and that thou hast loved them even as thou hast loved me" (Jn 17,22-23).

The experience of fraternal unity and active participation in the testimony of faith in the mystery of unity is a token of the eternal beatifying participation in the love mystery of God, one and three: "Father, I will that where I am, they also whom thou hast given me may be with me; in order that they may behold my glory, which thou hast given me, because thou hast loved me before the creation of the world" (Jn 17,24).

The Council and the High Priestly Prayer

The grand theme of the Second Vatican Council is the Church. She ponders her own nature, her mission, and her forms of life in the light of her own basic mystery and seeks to renew herself in such a manner that all can recognize that truly the Lord uttered the high priestly prayer for her, and that it is she who is the community of the faithful disciples bound by the double commandment of love. The Church examines her conscience. She inquires and must inquire whether or not her whole structure and vesture, her liturgy, her preaching of the faith, her moral message, and her judicial forms are stamped by the mystery of unity and love, whether they are calculated in the present hour of salvation to serve the testimony of this mystery.

The Church would be altogether too much of this world if she were to be conceived first of all and most of all in the juridical bond of unity. Certainly, the Church is in this world. For that very reason she needs a visible organization. She needs laws and administrative regulations. But if she wishes to remain faithful to her essence and to give comprehensible and authentic testimony, she must view all this as merely a manifestation of her most intimate mystery. If the Church makes use of the powerful means of this world for the conservation of her unity and the integrity of the faith—inquisition, temporal power, privileges which essentially are not a service but a being served—then she must be weak. She obscures her mission and robs herself of her true and proper power of attraction. The Church of the Second Vatican Council must be fully determined to put aside all juridical vestures and practices which are not suitable for her task of bringing her message to the world of today.

If our Pontiff John of the Second Vatican Council wished and hoped for the assembly of the world episcopate to become a wonderful drama of unity and love, an invitation to all to participate in the mystery of unity, by that fact he united himself to the confident cry with which the heart of the Savior closed His high priestly prayer: "Just Father, the world has not known thee, but I have known thee, and these have known that thou hast sent me. And I have made known to them thy name, and will make it known, in order that the love with which thou hast loved me may be in them, and I in them" (Jn 17,25-26).

II

THE CONCERNS OF THE COUNCIL
IN THE LIGHT OF THE MYSTERY
OF UNITY

The greater the awareness of purpose on the part of the fathers and the faithful, united to the conciliar effort with their prayers and sacrifices and eagerly awaiting the opportunity to carry out the directives, the more clearly the outlines of the principal designs of the Council will take shape. The more faithfully they hold in their minds and cherish in their hearts the grand mystery of unity, the more objectively the principal perspectives will emerge. Only a few days before the inauguration of the Council, one of the cardinals had this to say of the objectives: "We are entering a tunnel, and no one knows where it leads." Now, after the opening discourse of John XXIII and the first session of the Council, we see our way much more clearly.

It is now quite apparent that the directive words of the Holy Father have proved fruitful from the very first. For those few who had the notion that the Council should be occupied above all with as comprehensive as possible a condemnation of errors and the repudiation of the less tenable scholastic opinions, the words of the Pope came like a bolt from the blue. Gossip at Rome carried the tale that a certain prelate exclaimed spontaneously after the opening session to another prelate, "The Pope could not or dare not say that," to which the other replied, "Monsignor, but he did say it!" His words are of such far-reaching significance and historical import that it is worth our while to examine our conciliar anticipations and desires in the light of the Pope's words. The allocution of the Pontiff has given the Council its direction, the spiritual unity of its goals; to these it must turn. The bishops have striven with courage, patience, and love to make this directive fruitful.

Awareness of the Faith in the Sign of the Mystery of Unity

The forces working for the reconstruction of the unity of the family of Christ, and with the same purpose in mind for the return of all men of good will to the unity of the one holy, catholic, and apostolic Church, cannot slight the unity of truth. In fact, the great mystery of unity is resplendent in all the truths of salvation. This objective reality was clearly expressed in these words of the Holy Father, which echo the thought of St. Paul: that according to the design of God, "who wishes all men to be saved and to come to the knowledge of the truth" (I Tm 2,4), men cannot, without the aid of the entire revealed doctrine, arrive at a deep and solid unity of minds and hearts, with which true peace and eternal salvation is bound up. In preparing the general atmosphere of love and goodness and in proclaiming at the same time the entire revealed truth to the men of today, the Church serves this sublime goal of unity. "Sad to relate, however, the entire Christian family has not yet attained full and perfect visible unity in truth."

We cannot fail to detect the considerate approach in this

formulation of the Pontiff's thought. He begins with the fact that all Christians, all the baptized, form in a most real sense *one family*. It is a family, however, which is still only on the way toward "visible unity in truth." The Church is not motivated by ruthless fanaticism for truth; the very heart of the Christian message of truth, the mystery of unity, obliges the Church to proclaim the entire truth—neither more nor less—with the greatest love: "The Catholic Church considers it her duty to strive earnestly for the fulfillment of the great mystery of that unity for which Christ Jesus prayed so ardently to His heavenly Father on the eve of His sacrifice." Here we have come to the essential point of this very significant discourse of the Pope.

The entire Church, and in a uniquely tender way the Council, must therefore treat the truth in this hour of grace with the greatest love. It is not enough to set to work with simple zeal—with a forthright "unenlightened zeal"—for purely abstract truth. Instead, love for Him Who is for us the Truth and the Way to the truth must always be perceptible in our zeal; that is our zeal for truth must manifest love for Christ and full union with His love. Dealing with His love, love for redemptive truth and love for all men for whom He suffered and died, the messengers of truth must be constantly inspired and guided by love for those for whom the saving truth is destined. One who constantly brandishes truth in the face of another sins not only against his neighbor but also against truth itself and, yes, against Christ, the eternal Word of the Father, Who is Truth, that Truth which breathes forth Love, the Holy Spirit, and penetrates our souls with a divine pedagogy through love.

Christ's magisterium is the teaching office of the pastor who does not strike his sheep but calls each by name.

The flame of love for the separated brethren, so marvelously enkindled by Pope John XXIII, is an authentic aid to a more profound penetration into revealed truths. Moreover, it is an entirely essential prerequisite for the happy formulation of revealed truths in the face of the needs and the yearnings of our time. When John, the beloved disciple, admonished, "He who does not love does not know God; for God is love" (I Jn 4,8), he did not mean only love for the invisible God. He had in mind precisely that love which is inseparable, love for God and for one's fellows, which we see in Jesus Christ Who is incarnate Love. He meant that living love of the invisible God which was made possible to us through the visible appearance of the Word of God in the flesh and through our love for our visible brethren in union with Christ.

Vital proclamation of the eternal Truth, vital theology, exists only where faith is at work as well as hope and love.

An anti-Protestant complex, or for that matter an anti-Eastern bias or any other disdainful bearing toward the men of our time, must have catastrophic results in the formulation of the truth. This holds good not merely because such an attitude would render disservice to unity but also because revealed truth itself would be disfigured. Is not revealed truth inherently and of its own intrinsic purpose truth unto the salvation of all—something which is impossible if it is robbed of the splendor of love?

The truth certainly has been entrusted to the Church to be conserved in all its purity, but this does not mean that it was given her to be embalmed in dead formulas or merely shut up in a citadel and defended by anathemas. The truth has been entrusted to the Church to be announced as vital truth, to be formulated always in the most vital and vitalizing intelligible manner, to all men of all times and of every culture. It is likewise true that the conservation of the patrimony of the faith in all its integrity presupposes respect for the ancient documents and their painstaking study. But we must bear in mind that the formulation of these documents reflects the vivid dialogue of a particular epoch and culture, and that therefore it cannot be grasped perfectly if consideration is not given to the terms of that dialogue. But this is the decisive point—the conservation of the integrity is guaranteed by living tradition, that is to say, through vital and loving fulfillment of the proclamation in the service permeated with love for the mystery of unity in truth, in witness to the Church vivified by the Holy Spirit.

The Pope was fully aware of the impotence of force and a purely negative attitude toward those who are in error. Sympathetic understanding prompted him to state his "Johannine message" in these terms: "Under [today's] circumstances, the Catholic Church as she raises aloft the torch of religious truth through this Ecumenical Council seeks to show herself the loving mother of all men, kindly, patient, and filled with mercy and goodness toward the children separated from her."

The Holy Father opposed any reversion to the rigor and severity sometimes employed in the formulation of anathemas in the past: "But in this present age the Spouse of Christ prefers to apply the balm of mercy, rather than

take up the arms of severity and punishment. She is convinced that present day needs are more wisely served by explaining the value of her doctrine more fully than by condemning the errors which contradict it."

Pope John trusted the persuasive and convincing power of
the proclamation of the saving truth in a formulation inspired by love. He went further in directly and clearly expressing his hope that this loving manner of rethinking the
mystery of salvation in the service of unity will also effect
progress in the development of doctrine.

What is needed at the present time is that the whole Christian doctrine in its integrity be universally accepted with renewed zeal and with peaceful and tranquil minds. . . . What is
required and what all sincere lovers of the Christian Catholic
apostolic ideal ardently crave is that this same doctrine be more
widely known and more deeply understood and that men's spirits
be more fully imbued with it and formed in it. It is essential
that this doctrine . . . be studied and explained in accordance
with the needs of our own age.

This pastoral preoccupation with the exercise of the
teaching office orientates all theology to the kerygma, to
kerygmatic theology. From the point of view of the doctrinal
magisterium of the Church and of the theology itself placed
in her service, we cannot divorce the one saving truth with
which we must always remain in full accord from the hearer
to whom we must communicate it, now, here, today, for his
salvation. We cannot have an authentic theology in our
time without dialogue with contemporary men. This holds
for all to whom we announce the revealed truth: the faithful of today, the separated brethren, and even ourselves—
simply all men. We must search to know it with the

thought and idiom of our time and our culture. Because it is necessary to anchor our existence ever more profoundly in the truth, we must strive to make the truth our own and live it and proclaim it vitally.

There is therefore a concern for our own personal Christian life and our apostolate in the Pope's explicit invitation to us to reflect on the need for the authentic doctrine to be studied and propounded in the light of modern research and in the language of the present day. Anyone who is informed regarding the disputes of recent years will realize the profound grasp of reality in the following words:

It is essential that this doctrine, certain and immutable, to which we owe dutiful acceptance be studied and explained in accordance with the needs of our own age. The deposit of faith itself or the truths which is contained in our time-honored teaching is one thing; the manner in which it is set forth, in full integrity of sense and meaning, is another. Indeed, much consideration must be devoted to this manner of presentation, and if need be a painstaking effort must be made to elaborate it. This is to say that ways and means of exposition must be sought which are more in harmony with the magisterium whose character is predominantly pastoral.

How grateful must be our acknowledgment to the supreme Teacher of Christianity! The experiences of the past make us doubly thankful that in this historic hour he rejected the conception, so hazardous for the faith and for salvation, that we can conserve the faith integrally only if the truth be entirely crystallized in invariable formulas and forms and therefore, wherever possible, be sealed up in a dead language.

In stressing that the formulation of the message must be

lovingly open to the contemporary manner of thinking, the Pope enunciated the fundamental principle that the doctrinal magisterium as such is to be viewed in its pastoral function, indeed; as the expression of pastoral love. The teaching office of the Church is living tradition communicating the message of salvation. Such a magisterium demonstrates its fidelity in the proclamation of the message of the risen Lord by announcing the Gospel message to all peoples of all times in a dynamic manner which imparts to them its vital power.

The diffusion of sacred doctrine is essentially and entirely a service of love rendered by Christ through the Church to men of all times. It is therefore evident that the men of the Church and particularly the Council cannot perform this service well without a great reverence for the dignity of man and a loving recognition of the good will already present in men to whom they speak. Such respect, coupled with a Christian optimism, is evident in every phrase of the discourse with which John XXIII opened the Second Vatican Council. For example, note how confident he was that of themselves men today seem to condemn errors and specifically those forms and customs of life which scorn God and His laws. Beginning with the God-given conviction of the dignity of man, the Church bestows "the gifts of supernatural grace, which since they elevate men to the dignity of sons of God, are genuine defense and assistance in making their life more fully human. She opens the fountains of her life-giving doctrine so that illumined by the light of Christ men may fully understand what they really are, how exalted is their dignity, what goals they must seek." About modern men to whom the Church must turn today, the Pope said, "It is becoming increasingly evident that the dignity of the human person and true self-revelation are subjects of great moment and most difficult to achieve." We should note the loving gratitude to God with which the Pontiff spoke of the mystery of unity already at work in the prayers of the separated brethren and in the good will manifested even by non-Christians toward the Catholic Church; here one feels reverence for God externally manifested in respect for the partners in dialogue, a respect which not only induces men to speak but which also makes them listen, listen humbly and sincerely.

With the same confident Christian optimism manifest in the grand directive lines of the Pope and in the first acts of the fathers at the Council, we are permitted to hope that the fathers and all the theologians and the messengers of the word of God will adhere to this directive constantly and make it increasingly their own. Only if all are totally committed to the great mystery of unity and love and guided by it in their thoughts, their discussion, their writing, and their work can we anticipate the "step forward toward a penetration of doctrine and conscience formation willed by God."

Pope John of the Second Vatican Council taught in a most practical and convincing manner the primacy of charity in theological reflection and above all in the preaching and teaching of sacred doctrine. In the past, bitter controversies among the various schools of theology often deflected attention and energy from the pastoral needs of preaching and instructing and hampered true progress in theological research. Lack of charity produced unfavorable results in theology. There is always urgent need for dialogue filled with charity. The bishops, who are models in the Church for the theologians, must enter into loving dialogue. Only a dialogue among many who are endowed by God with the most diverse gifts, men of the most diverse culture —with a variety of languages bearing effective witness to the one Spirit—only this dialogue, filled with love in authentic Catholicity of unity and multiplicity, will serve to achieve union among Christians and to effect the conversion of non-Christians. And only this dialogue will lead to a profounder penetration of revealed truth itself.

As we see it, the results of the first session of the Council in this regard are unquestionably positive, even though it has as yet produced no dogmatic constitution. Note the following points:

1. The Council has clearly and decisively said no to those who wished to restrict it to favoring any scholastic theory whatsoever. The preservation of the faith integrally demands the greatest prudence in decisions regarding theories which within the Catholic Church—in the West or in the East—were and are objects of controversy among theologians and the theological schools of the orthodox faith.

2. The pastoral character of the forms of dogmatic utterance has been decisively advanced not as an accessory point of view but as an essential demand of revealed truth, the truth of salvation and of the doctrinal magisterium of the Church.

It has been noted that theology which conceives its own nature and scope in such a way that it is bereft of pastoral interest can be considered as buried once and for all.

4. The primacy of charity—and this is a characteristic mode of thought from the standpoint of the mystery of love —is demanded also for dogmatic doctrinal proclamation. Such a demand is manifested in the most classical manner by the allocution the Holy Father delivered at the end of the first session, in which he expressed his joy over the fact that up to that time all the endeavors of the Council had made charity visible in truth. Charity, the saving mystery of love, is not annexed externally to the other saving truths but is the very warmth of their heart and the glow of their countenance.

4

The Moral Message of the Church

John XXIII is a personification of the Johannine primacy of love, not merely in his utterances but also and particularly in his actions and in the uniqueness of his personality. And though he placed pastoral love and the mystery of unity in the very center of the general proclamation of the truths of faith, the stress is doubly marked in his enunciation of the moral message of the Church. It is quite apparent how much he had at heart the proclamation of this message. Even more important to him was the realization of the joyful news in *action*. This unity of proclamation and action can be noted throughout the papal utterances. Let us take as an example these words from the opening discourse: "Everywhere through her children she enlarges the frontiers of Christian love, for nothing is so effective in eradicating the seeds of discord and promoting harmony, peace, justice, and universal brotherhood."

We may therefore confidently hope that the fathers of the Council called together by John will not be content to propose a simple catalogue of individual precepts and fundamental principles in the areas of moral practice or merely enunciate a list of anathemas against the errors of our time.

The renewal of Christian life can spring solely from the deep fountain of the unity which is triune in God's love for Himself. The moral message of Christianity will be the more efficacious the more clearly it testifies to the mystery of unity and love and the more profoundly it is inspired by this mystery even in its formulation. The moral message of the Church must be *praeconium paschale*, the paschal announcement, reaching out to the end of all ages, a paschal message which is joyful, glorifying, and expressive of the triumphant love of Christ. It is the message of the cross and the resurrection.

The renewal of Catholic moral theology and of the moral sermon means basically a conscious return to the scriptural and patristic approach in announcing the Good News of the Christian life. In the last several decades considerable progress has been made in this area, thanks above all to the biblical movement and the liturgical renewal. But much still remains to be done before that perilous attitude of mind—quite widespread among the faithful—can be overcome, a state which merited the rebuke of Paul Claudel: "Certainly we love Christ, but nothing in the world can lead us to love the moral."[1]

There are no currents of thought in the Catholic Church which contain an explicit denial of the truth that on the dual commandment of love for God and for one's neigh-

---

[1] To Claudel *the moral* meant moralism, something widely diffused among Christians that chills Christian life and robs it of true joy.

bor "depend the whole Law and the Prophets" (Mt 22,40). But it does seem that moralists and preachers of morals at times simply overlook this truth. Sometimes the primacy of love is obscured because principal stress is placed on individual commandments and requirements or on an abstractive, objective order and its claims rather than on the God of love. At times some seem to think it sufficient to stress this truth incidentally, or to reserve it for asceticism and mysticism. Others even maintain that it is hazardous to place consistent emphasis on this truth.

At certain moments in history, so great was the concern for a solution of all possible moral cases together with a condemnation of all possible moral aberrations and errors in complete and total detail that the primacy of love was almost totally neglected. Authors involved in such procedures were quite ready to cite St. John, "He who has my commandments and keeps them, he it is who loves me" (Jn 14,21), to prove that in the last analysis everything depends on the externally correct observance of the many commandments rather than on some sort of *sentiment* of love. This love, they maintained, could not be strictly defined or clearly marked by boundaries of legal obligations. Hence it could not be strictly imposed.

But in all this two points were slighted. First, the Lord Himself in the passage preceding the text just cited expressly explained that love for Him is not sentiment, though it is without doubt the font from which flows the fulfillment of His commandments: "If you love me, keep my commandments" (Jn 14,15). He adds that He will send the Spirit of truth to assist them (Jn 14,16ff). And it is

Jesus Himself who through His vivifying Spirit, Who is Love, shares with us His own love and renders us capable of love in return. Second, in the context of the parting discourse at the Last Supper and of the high priestly prayer, the term commandment does not indicate primarily a multiplicity of single moral duties but rather the entire personal charge of the Savior to us, the intensity of the Lord's demand for our whole self, the urgent invitation to love Him and with Him the Father and to observe in that love His new commandment, "that as I have loved you, you also love one another" (Jn 13,34).

In the same breath Jesus speaks of His commandments He gives to us and the commandments His heavenly Father imposes upon Him. As everything for Jesus is summed up in His love for the Father and in the charge received from the Father to bring men divine love on the concrete and human level, so too Jesus embraces us in His love for the Father and in His love for all. The commandments in the sense of the Gospel of John are above all a living faith, a joyous and thankful acceptance of the redemptive truth, and also loving gratitude as the response to the love of the Lord. This living, grateful faith is the source of the perfect good in every respect. It is fulfillment in love flowing from love. This obviously does not imply that the Christian must make an express intention before every act, directing it by a motive of love to God. But love which ultimately motivates every individual intention must progressively animate all our aspirations.

To avoid the fragmentation of moral teaching into a disorganic plurality of duties and laws, there must be a re-

capitulation of the individual commandments in the great
commandment of love for God and for one's fellows. Such
a recapitulation must above all be the serious concern of us
Catholics and in fact of all Christians. The more clearly
the Council leads and directs us to this awareness, the
more will we progress toward the union of Christians and
toward the conversion of the world to the Church.

In keeping with these considerations, it might be profit-
able to reflect on a misgiving known to be current among
the people of the Eastern churches: the fear of being legally
pressured into Westernization. Past centuries do bear evidence of such pressures. Their existence in the West is disturbing. Similarly, we should not make light of the Protestant fears that Protestant Christians are to be Romanized.
(Some call this a Pauline misgiving.) The Council called
together by Pope John is in a position to dispel such
anxieties and concerns. It needs only to follow the Johannine line of the Pontiff and spell out its formulations entirely in the light and the spirit of the primacy of love.

Regarding the juridical positivism of many of our contemporaries and the Nominalistic undercurrents present
even in the Christian camp, we must make our position
completely clear in this historic moment; all man's duties
are an effusion of the wisdom and the loving will of God,
Who manifests the law of His wisdom above all through
His gift of Himself. The Father gives His Word, the Incarnate Word Who sends the Spirit from the Father. In
the Christian moral life this mystery of the Trinity is at
work. The triune God works within us openly and effectively. Our moral instruction must be filled with this

mystery. "The new covenant is a covenant of the Holy Spirit, 'because the charity of God is poured forth by the Holy Spirit who has been given to us' (Rom 5,5). And He is the new covenant insofar as He produces in us charity, which is the fulfillment of the Law."[2]

The Catholic Church today is in a special manner open to the *law of the Spirit*, as St. Paul proclaims it and as the great Doctors of the Church—Augustine, Thomas, and all others who share their noble spirit—explicitly propounded it. Augustine wrote, "What are the commandments of God, written in our hearts by God Himself, if not the grace of the Holy Spirit through whose presence there is infused in our hearts that charity which is the fullness of the Law?"[3]

A merely external coordination of the commandments around charity, a mere focusing of attention externally on charity as the motive, a structuring of commandments with charity set on a parallel line alongside so many other commandments, is not sufficient. In every part of our preaching and instruction regarding the moral message we must be aware of that which is the distinctive mark and sign of the moral ideal of the New Testament—charity, "the law of the Spirit of the life in Christ Jesus" (Rom 8,2); and we must interiorize the law, the single, twofold commandment of love which is the fullness of the whole law through the effusion of the Holy Spirit.

The mysterious character of this interiorization was al-

[2] St. Thomas Aquinas, *Commentary on II Corinthians 3*, Lesson 2.

[3] St. Augustine, *De Spiritu et littera*, cap. 21; PL 44, 222.

ready foretold by the prophet Jeremia in the Old Testament: "But this is the covenant which I will make with the house of Israel after those days, says the Lord: 'I will place my law within them, and write it upon their hearts" (Jer 31,33; see Heb 8,10). The prophet Ezechiel touches the mystery more closely; repeatedly he has God speak of a "new heart" and a "new spirit" which He will pour forth in the time of the fullness of grace (Ez 11,19; 18,31). The decisive word, however, is that God will give us His own Spirit: "And I will give you a new heart, and place a new spirit within you, taking from your bodies your stony hearts and giving you natural hearts. I will put my spirit within you and make you live by my statutes, careful to observe my decrees" (Ez 36,26-27).

Through the inspiration and operation of the Holy Spirit, the will and work of baptized man participate in the great mystery of unity. The Spirit overcomes every division and separation. He places on man the seal of unity, the principle of love that animates all action and struggle, whether it be in the individual or in the community.

Placing clearly in relief the most profound mystery of Christian morality and the primacy of grace also dams up in the most effective way the certainly perilous currents of mundane laicist morality. These constitute a real threat even to our faithful today. In fact, we may say they are a greater hazard than any of the particular errors which are a menace to one or another individual commandment of God.

The formidable currents of contemporary thought, existentialism and collectivism, must be purged and purified by the mystery of unity. All that is in them of life, all that is pregnant and meaningful, can be taken up, redeemed, and rendered efficacious in a higher synthesis. And this higher synthesis is the vision of the whole of life in the function of the mystery of unity, which here on earth is manifested through the Spirit, the Lord and Lifegiver, in His multiplicity of gifts and vocations.

A sound existentialism—and even its degeneration into an erroneous situation ethics—contains some Christian elements. It represents an antithesis to the stereotyped, the pallid, and the legalistic. It seeks to lift man from the anonymous soulless mass or collectivity. A merely negative condemnation, especially if it is couched in juridical and abstract forms, will not succeed in shattering the hold or destroying the fascination of a misguided existentialism. But even given this fascination, existentialism's stress on liberty and the necessity of risk in morality must appear as meaningless gibberish to men who have grasped the significance of the liberty of God's children living in perfect obedience to "the law of the Spirit of the life in Christ Jesus" (Rom 8,2), according to the unfathomable riches of the gifts of grace. And yet, a legalism which is capable only of presenting the law of the Lord as uniformity under a yoke imposed from without or which conceives obedience too much as a mechanical application of general formulas is most likely to turn an even greater number of men to false existentialism. And instead of meeting and expanding the possibilities for good in the spirit of the age, it will share responsibility for its degeneration.

Collectivism, above all Marxist collectivism, which rep-

resents such terrifying power, may be at least partially explained as a reaction to a narrow egoism and individualism
regarding salvation in the Christian West. Even com-
munism is not completely lacking in elements basically
Christian, though these elements are evident only to the
eyes of love and do not free Marxism from condemnation. Condemnation is not lacking; in fact, Marxism is in
many respects its own condemnation. But the misery on
which it thrives and which we must overcome is corrected
only through exemplary realization of those values which
Marxism secretly and ardently craves, even though in the
utterly false collectivist vision. Christian moral must cul-
tivate community perspectives more fully. The truth of the
community of salvation, of the solidarity of all in Christ,
in the ultimate analysis the truth of the great mystery of
love, must become clearly visible in moral preaching and
instruction, in the forms of the life of Christians, and in
the structures of ecclesiastical life.

Degenerate existentialism sacrifices fidelity, stability, and
unity of life for a misconceived individualistic and isolated
liberty. Collectivism sacrifices the riches of the human
person and the variety of human dispositions for an ex-
aggerated organization and external conformity.

The vision of the moral life in the light of the mystery
of unity demands the greatest acceptance of liberty—of
liberty conceived as participation in divine liberty, and
therefore embracing the divine directive in the gift of God
—but always on the level of saving solidarity. Person and
community are mutually enriching. True community rests
on a multiplicity of gifts, functions, and characters and on

true maturity and spontaneity in the person. The decisive bond of unity is not merely organization and legislation but also love and mutual respect.

The relation to temporal things must also be considered in the mystery of unity. Are we not concerned above all with the redemption of all things, a return of all in and through Christ?—Christ "who descended, he it is who ascended also above all the heavens, that he might fill all things" (Eph 4,10). The Church cannot hope to lead modern man "to the unity of the faith and of the deep knowledge of the Son of God" (Eph 4,13) without introducing into his cultural and spiritual world the light of faith and the flame of Christian charity. The Church cannot limit herself to a mere negative and cautionary attitude; she cannot make it her principal task to put men on guard against the hazards of modern technology, sociology, psychology, or restrict her efforts to the condemnation of individual opinions that are dangerous.

Regarding this point we must not confuse the task of the Holy Office, whose competence is principally in the function of surveillance, and equate it simply with the teaching magisterium. A clear distinction is necessary in order both to view the Holy Office with its special tasks in a just light and—what is of particular importance—to avoid degrading the solemn role of the magisterium of the Council to pure surveillance and conservation. Such a caution, of course, by no means implies that the Council should not also make a clear statement pointing out the menace of certain actual dangerous tendencies.

It would be fatal if the Church of the Second Vatican

Council were to produce no more than severe admonitions or warnings regarding, for example, modern depth psychology. This would create the impression that she deals with the actual demands, methods, and experiences of this new science only as a suspicious and mistrustful critic. The same holds true for all the modern sciences with their decisive influence on the destiny of the world.

A purely negative position, a position of corrective aloofness or rejection on the part of the Church would signify in practice an abandonment of the world to others who do not possess the light of the faith. It has been maintained that "To invite men to shun error and evil is always an invitation to man's mind and heart to cling positively to truth and goodness."[4] The statement is dogmatically exact in the sense that in all her condemnations and admonitions the Church pursues such goals. But the magisterium, which is predominantly pastoral in character, must also heed the matters of right balance, proper proportion, and integration of goals, and, not least important, must have a regard for the laws of moral psychology and pedagogy. The dimensions of the Church's proclamation must be those of the Gospel. Admonitions and condemnations must derive their positive and meaningful purpose from the joyful message of the mystery of love. Should they on the contrary be isolated from or even obscure the Gospel, then they would inevitably arouse repugnance and rebellion in psychological reaction. A primarily negative presentation of the Church's message cannot be an attractive invitation or inducement to

[4] E. Lio, "Il lavoro del Concilio," *Osservatore Romano*, December 8, 1962, p. 2.

accept her moral doctrine with love. To speak truthfully, it mars the very countenance of the Church.

Failure to integrate the prohibitions of evil into the message of love combined with a presentation of the rules of life in negative formulas in Catholic manuals of moral (and hence in the care of souls) accounts in part for the loss of the masses to the Church. It helps explain why the modern world has sought guidance elsewhere. The admonitions of the Pope of the Council are particularly valid for the proclamation of moral doctrine. These admonitions may all be summed up in the one ideal of renewal in the spirit of the Gospel, in the spirit of the glad tidings.

The schema on the moral order proposed to the fathers of the Council was not taken up for discussion in the first session, but it was discussed very thoroughly by many groups of bishops. From the printed accounts of the content of the schema published by the Council, it is impossible to form a judgment on its content and directive line. However, we know that it belonged to those schemata which must be restudied and re-elaborated between the first and second sessions in accordance with the guidelines of the Council. Gradually the latter are assuming greater clarity and definition.

The first session of the Council introduced very clear and concrete bases and perspectives for the further development of Catholic moral theology. We should note the following points.

1. The discussion on the sources of revelation has confirmed the biblical renewal. Similarly, the constitution on the liturgy, already accepted unanimously in substance, as-

sures for the word of God an outstanding place of honor in joyous festal celebration. The decision can be no different regarding the proclamation of moral: it will be newly inspired by the Gospel, by the great perspectives of sacred Scripture, more than in previous centuries.

2. The deeper penetration into the doctrine of tradition has inflicted a mortal wound on the arid conceptualism which attempts to reduce tradition more or less to a handful of formulas. With the fathers of the Second Vatican Council we must view tradition principally as a vital current of truth under the influence of the presence of Christ and the operation of the Holy Spirit, as the life of the Church in the celebration of the sacred mysteries and her saints, as the concert of gifts of grace, and as the offices of shepherds and faithful people. If we view tradition thus, then the comprehension of the moral tradition of the Church will also gain in depth and richness by intrinsic necessity.

3. The sharp emphasis on revealed truth as the truth of salvation, on *caritas in veritate* (love in truth), and on the primacy of love in dogmatic theology assures moral instruction of that same decisive vision. Moreover—and this is not a negligible matter—the baneful divorce of dogma from moral theology will thus be healed.

4. No one has ever questioned the necessity of juridical elements in the structure of the Church, but it has been expressly emphasized that the juridical must be totally animated by love, by the great mystery of unity. It is unthinkable that in the total manifestation of the Church a more vital and more profound comprehension of the duties and laws based on mystery, service, and charity could effect a

breakthrough without a corresponding influence on the presentation of Catholic moral.

5. The first act of the Council, the liturgical renewal, views Christian life in the light of the salvation mystery, the mystery of grace whereby we are transformed in Christ. The Church hopes that because of this sacred renewal Christians, now more aware than in times past, will manifest in their lives and make known to others the mysteries of Christ and the true nature of the Church. Active and vital participation in the liturgy is the most powerful impulse for the faithful to "keep in their life what they have perceived by faith."[5] The comprehension of the Christian life within the framework of the celebration of the salvation mysteries is the most efficacious remedy for the current *malaise* of laistic morality, which is a grave menace even to the faithful in the Church.

[5] Oration for the Tuesday of Paschal Week.

The Liturgy and the Mystery of Faith

Not by chance did the Council begin its labors with its consultations on the schema of the liturgy, said Pope John. In the liturgy the Church's intimate mystery of love is revealed. Here she is encompassed and sanctified by the grand mystery of unity. United with Christ, all the members of the Church experience their unity in her and with one another. From the sacrifice and the sacraments the Church always receives in a new and grace-giving manner the commission and the power to bear witness; in community and in all her members she bears witness to the mystery of unity and love which is already active here on earth, redeeming and sanctifying.

All the sacraments, and in a most special way baptism, penance, and the eucharist, signify, as grace boldly proclaimed and as commitment experienced in the common faith, the unity of the people of God in the praise and glory of the triune love of God and the salvation of the world. The manner and degree in which the faith is expressed and proclaimed in the liturgy through common and vital worship are the measure according to which the mystery of unity is gratefully accepted and announced to all through the testimony of love in life.

The liturgical renewal faced so boldly by the Council proposes as its goal above all a greater encounter of the people of God with the mystery of faith and charity. The result should be a stronger, deeper faith penetrated with a holier reverence. Thus, the people of God are to be made aware of the royal road of love. It must be for them much more than a simple humanitarian love of mankind and more than a simple commandment. Only the mystery of faith, vital and powerful, points effectively and correctly to the mystery of unity and love. If the whole Council has as its task to render the message of faith more accessible to our contemporaries—to men of all cultures—without attenuation and with profound penetration, the living celebration of the liturgy will serve as nothing else would to accomplish that task. The living faith manifesting itself in the liturgy, ever glowing, ever inflaming, will move Christians to bear witness to their faith and charity, a testimony which is authentic and triumphant.

It appears to be a baneful error, prejudicial to souls, to hold that the liturgy must almost by necessity be celebrated in a dead idiom, as though certain parts must be kept from the minds of the faithful. Surprisingly indeed, the express purpose of this crystallization is to preserve the integrity of the liturgy. But the faith is not a talent which may be buried. It is life in the Holy Spirit. Only faith which is vitally grasped, vitally celebrated, and hence vitally experienced can be conserved in its integrity and power. If the celebration of the sacred mysteries is not alive but vague and incomprehensible, if there is a wall between liturgical participation of a purely sentimental kind and catechesis which is merely doctrinal, then the faith of the Christian community and its testimony to the faith will necessarily be fatally languid. Formulations of scholastic theology, no matter how precise, and condemnations of error in faith, no matter how comprehensive and severe, cannot effectively prevent the loss of faith. The danger of mass apostasy still remains.

If the liturgical renewal is carried out according to the design of the fathers of the Council with a true interior spirit of renewal, with the will of spiritual renewal and continuous conversion, then the result will be a great blessing—a blessing of unity in the Church. The faithful gathered around the altar, celebrating the sacred mysteries in a manner accessible to their minds as well as to their mode of life, can better understand that they form one family of God. They can realize that precisely as a special living brotherhood—the family, the parish, and the like— they are an image of the whole Church. The most eloquent and the most beatifying celebration of the great mystery of love will be for them a constant appeal to the realization that they are one in the great family of the holy Church with all of Christ's redeemed.

The very diversity of liturgical languages and forms should make the essential structure of the liturgy, which should always be preserved intact, all the more conspicuous. A loving consideration of the very existence of many languages and cultures should focus attention on the riches of the Church's catholicity. Catholicity in breadth and depth must impress men's consciousness deeply and convincingly. The unity of the Mystical Body of Christ bears no resemblance to the dead conformism of a collectivist dictatorship, for its rich and diversified unity is itself a joyful acknowledgment of the magnificent variation in gift and vocation—natural and supernatural—of individual and community. The renewed liturgy of the rites of Latin origin should produce a nobler harmony with the other ancient rites, promising new developments, which are indispensable for the worldwide apostolate of the Church.

Only in this way will the one great liturgy of the Catholic Church of the Orient and the Occident become in keeping with I Corinthians 11-14, a constant and perceptible praise of the Spirit. It will speak the praise of the Spirit Who distributes the diversity of gifts, functions, and tasks and thereby binds all with the same bond of charity. It will speak in praise of the one same Spirit "who allots to everyone according as he will" (I Cor 12,11).

Latin as the language of the liturgy consumed an entire week of open and frank discussion in the Council, which surely was not futile. Some of the quips about Latin provoked universal amusement. Strangely enough they were first spoken in dead earnest: "Where Latin dies, the Church is already dead"; "A single step away from Latin is a step toward schism."[1] These jests unintentionally furthered a good cause. Now that the Council has struck the golden mean and thereby come upon a totally unanticipated concert of opinion among the world's bishops, Latin will be able to render a humble but eagerly welcomed service for

[1] See *Informations Catholiques Internationales*, no. 181 (1962), p. 13.

the unity of the Church. It has an important role to play as the language of administration, as an indispensable key to the treasures of tradition, and as an element in the liturgy. However, it cannot represent the unity of which we have been speaking, above all not in the liturgical celebration.

Latin will help conserve the unity of the Roman rite in the midst of all the lawful multiplicity. The Orientals, who of course have always celebrated their own marvelous liturgy in other idioms and thereby turned their attention rather to the comprehension of the people, will be able to breathe freely as though emancipated from an ancient yoke after the new regulations are put into operation. Never again should they have reason to be fearful that they are considered, despite all assurances to the contrary, as less intimately bound up in the common unity of the Church because they do not pray in Latin or accept Occidental forms of religious expression. The Church of the Second Vatican Council, having come to see with extraordinary clarity that her Latin vesture has become too tight, has thereby removed another obstacle to the return of Protestant Christians. She is now more universally and therefore better prepared for the mission of redeeming every culture and every language in the one orchestration for the praise and glory of the mystery of unity.

A further step toward *rapprochement* between the Orient and the Occident and toward razing the walls between them is indicated in the suggestion of certain changes in the Latin rite: the granting of permission for full concelebration of priests, and the granting of the chalice to the laity. As to both points it should be noted that the concelebration of priests, particularly with their own bishop, and the laity's reception of holy communion under both species are profound symbolic representations of holy unity. Merely to read in a theological tract or for that matter in a catechism that the eucharist signifies the unity of the one priesthood of Christ and the unity of all the sacerdotal people of God is less impressive than genuine concelebration of the one sacrifice. In impressive concelebration the faith of the one priesthood of Christ and the Church is more strikingly symbolized and experienced than in the individual celebrations at a number of separate altars at which groups gather, limiting their exercise of fraternal charity to a cautious avoidance of disturbing others by saying and attending mass in hushed whispers.

The liturgical devotion is a continuation of the visible experience of the presence of the incarnate Word, meeting us and dealing with us on our own level. It is the experience of faith, according to a well-known passage of St. Leo the Great: "*Quod Redemptoris nostri conspicuum fuit, in sacramenta transivit*," the visible manifestation of our Redeemer is continued and expressed in the sacred signs, the sacraments.[2] The eucharistic union of sacrifice and communion must enter into the experience of believing men insofar as this is possible. If we refuse to partake of food or drink with certain men and certain classes of men, then we establish an obstacle to union, an insurmountable wall of division.

There are no dogmatic or pastoral reasons founded on universal principles for a sweeping refusal to grant the

[2] St. Leo the Great, Sermon 72, PL 54, 389.

chalice to the laity in the Roman rite. In fact, the Roman Church from times past has permitted all the faithful, those of the Roman rite included, to receive holy communion under both species whenever they assist at a mass of another Catholic rite which follows this practice. Today no question of the true faith is involved, for no one is tempted to deny the presence of the whole Christ under either species. If, however, there is reason to fear that the faithful would be disturbed or have difficulty in a matter of faith because of some new regulation, then indeed there is no excuse for further delay in instructing them in a more profound and substantial comprehension of that same faith. At all times, and in none more urgently than in this age of pluralistic society, the Christian must be able to render an account of his faith. This clearly implies that he be capable of distinguishing the unchanging content of faith from passing forms of devotion.

As of now we do not know what decisions the Council will make regarding the concelebration of the mass and the granting of the chalice to the laity. Here, too, ecclesiastic tradition and pastoral care indicate that no abrupt and total change should be decided upon. The Church loves organic development and prudent transition. There will probably be permissions of this kind for very specific reasons and within clearly defined limits. But we have hope that the attitudes and the foundation of the new legislation will be perfectly in accord with the guidelines of the great mystery of unity.

6

THE COLLEGE OF BISHOPS
AND THE ROMAN CURIA

The Church of the Second Vatican Council looks at herself and asks herself how she represents the mystery of love and unity according to the intention of her divine Founder. The Church wishes to be faithful to that assignment, not merely in doctrinal decisions but also in her structures and life forms. The development of dogma takes place not merely through doctrinal definition but also and above all through increasing awareness of the fullness of life in a truth and through a more fruitful presentation of it in life's actualities extended into the area of juridical regulations.

One problem is unquestionably decisive: how indeed the office of Peter and his successors and the functions of the College of Bishops can effectively serve in the proclamation of the mystery of unity and love. The problem is fundamental. It also involves the question of fidelity to an historic task in this hour of grace.

The First Council of the Vatican rendered an important service to the internal unity of the Catholic Church with its clear definition and delineation of infallibility and of the primacy of jurisdiction of the successor of Peter. However, to view the prerogatives of the Roman Church primarily from the juridical standpoint or to consider the dogma of papal primacy and infallibility directly under the aspect of power and external force would obscure the service the dogma can render and totally falsify its significance. Spiritual power in general and that of St. Peter in particular must be decisively considered as *service*, as the authority of love, as the gift of love of Christ, Who "has not come to be served but to serve, and to give his life as a ransom for many" (Mt 20,28). The words are not incidental ascetic admonition but truly a reference to the most intimate function of spiritual power, with which the Lord cautions His disciples, ". . . let him who is greatest among you become as the youngest, and him who is the chief as the servant" (Lk 22,26).

Pope John XXIII has placed this truth in full light by his utterances and even more by his very person and actions. In the homily of the mass of his coronation, he clearly expressed his own conception of the fundamental meaning of humility in the spiritual office: "The center of divine instruction and the commandment which includes all others and supports them are the words of the Gospel: 'Learn from me, for I am meek and humble of heart'" (Mt 11,29). Conscious of the hazards for humility and for the will to serve in an overly human conception of the spiritual office, the Pope on that momentous occasion begged all pious men to pray for him unceasingly to help him progress in humility and the will to serve.

The exalted prerogatives of the Roman Church have as

their goal and purpose the service and profit of the universal Church as the community in the love of Christ. According to a frequently cited passage of St. Ignatius, Bishop and Martyr, the Roman Church is called to preside over the union of love. She possesses a primacy of charity. Not because of his merit or deserts but solely because of the free and undeserved love of Christ was Peter chosen. His mission did not derive from human legal claims but from the love of Christ. This is not at all to detract from the rights inherent in papal primacy but rather to place them in their proper setting and focus attention on their meaning and their effective exercise in the light of the primacy of love. To maintain a purely juridical primacy over love and its divine power would seem to me to be nothing less than heresy. On the other hand, to deny the juridical entirely in the name of love would be equally fatal.

The Church of the Word incarnate cannot renounce her juridical and administrative structure as expression of the community of love. But by force of her inner nature and her mission—to bear witness to the perennial love and the love-supremacy of Christ—the Church must constantly be preoccupied with adjusting all her changing structures to the actual needs of the community of love. She must balance all these changing forms with the actual and changing needs of the fellowship of love in the spirit of loving service to the point of self-abnegation. The structures constituted and determined by Christ are of themselves totally and utterly the expression of a mission which signifies service and love. This mission itself, of course, cannot undergo change.

If we take human frailty into account, we must always

be aware of the ever-present danger that the application and administration of Church law may in some way be looked upon as ends instead of means. Frail administrators are liable to follow the spirit of this world and the pattern of purely secular power, and in consequence may to a degree forfeit their noblest functions. Juridical institutions may in their origins be more or less in conformity with spiritual ends and adapted to the needs of a given age. However, they may become formal and rigid as time passes and become themselves the goals to which they are devoted. Certain juridical institutions like the ecclesiastical inquisition have tended from their very inception rather to obscure the primacy of charity.

The guidelines of the Johannine message are a guarantee that all the considerations of the Second Vatican Council regarding the Church, her constitution, and her direction will bear the stamp of the primacy of charity and service. Central to the study of the problem are principally two basic questions or groups of questions, which are not altogether mutually exclusive: (1) What is the relation of the pope to the College of Bishops? (2) What are the relations among the pope, the episcopate, and the Roman curia?

Papal Primacy Within the College of Bishops

The primacy of the pope must be considered as being within the College of Bishops, not parallel to it.

The First Vatican Council solemnly defined that the doctrinal decisions proposed to the universal Church by the pope, when he defines doctrine with full authority as the supreme pastor and teacher of the Church, are irreversible *in se*, that is, by his very authority, and not through the consent of the Church.[1] There is no appeal from the head of the apostolic College to a council or the College when the head, Peter, has spoken with supreme authority and with the intent of obliging the conscience of all.

From this definition, however, one cannot conclude that the pope, in the solemn moment when he exercises supreme authority, acts in isolation—if we may use the term—as one who is outside the apostolic College. He acts rather as head of the College of Bishops, to which he belongs entirely. He does not teach new doctrine, but solemnly proposes the teaching of sacred Scripture and the apostolic tradition. This he does not produce or invent but carefully and humbly investigates "as the times and circumstances suggest, whether it be by convoking ecumenical councils or by probing the mind of the Church dispersed over the world, or again by means of particular councils or by the use of other aids supplied by divine providence."[2] In the doctrinal and pastoral magisterium of Peter there is active at the same time the doctrinal and pastoral magisterium of the whole College of Bishops, though in a different manner. Not in submission of the head to the College but in solidarity with it does the pope speak. The solidarity is wrought by the Holy Spirit and conserved by the entire Church in union with Peter and in unanimous loyalty to the full apostolic tradition.

[1] Denz. (32) 3074.
[2] Denz. (32) 3069.

An explicit elaboration of the collegiate role of the bishops does not in fact imply a diminution of authority in the office of Peter. Quite the contrary, it focuses attention on the true plenitude of his power in relation to the bishops as a body. The pope's primacy of authority is not merely honorary, but it is not a form of dictatorship. He possesses the highest level of that authority which is the essential expression of the community of charity and its solidarity in the service of God and of souls; he presides over the College of Bishops and all the flock with the fullness of authority of the pastor of pastors. He is the supreme shepherd of the entire flock.

Historic developments of the past few centuries have directed the bishops almost exclusively into what we might call a vertical relation of individual prelate with the central authority of the Church. The episcopal conferences of entire nations, regions, and continents organized in more recent times, however, have become increasingly operative and effective. These surely mark a degree of progress. In this manner the bishops of one nation or of a distinct territory or the bishops using the same language cooperate more and more effectively on a common pastoral plane. They experience a fuller sense of solidarity, with the result that their care of souls reflects the mystery of unity more strikingly and clearly.

The episcopal conferences established in recent times already testify to authentic Catholic solidarity of worldwide dimensions. It is sufficient to point to the tremendously impressive work of the National Catholic Welfare Conference in the United States or to the two special forms of endeavor of the German episcopate, the Misereor and the Adveniat. A clear juridical delineation of the area of competence and duty of episcopal conferences should further their efficacious work appreciably. The result should be not only greater conformity on the pastoral level but also greater harmony in the relations between the various episcopal conferences on the one hand and the central authority of the Church on the other, which is to say that both unity and love would be greatly furthered.

An important achievement of the Second Vatican Council is the increase of solidarity of the bishops of the whole world gathered at Rome through their encounter. In full liberty and ardent charity, the bishops assemble around the successor of Peter. Wrestling with problems which affect the whole Church, they cannot fail to be profoundly aware of their unified role as the College of Bishops of the entire world, sharing in epoch-making decisions at a great moment of history. In this atmosphere the problems of their own dioceses are viewed in a more just prospective. Looking beyond the narrow horizon of their own nations, they see their particular responsibilities in the light of the common and universal duty. By common endeavor, one supporting the other, they discharge the duties of their office. They hearken to one another and learn from each other through an exchange of ideas. They even express their biases in their criticisms of the thoughts and decisions of the episcopacies of other countries. After the Council is over, their mutual love will be more understanding, more concrete and objective.

In this context we need only call to mind many loose,

superficial, and in fact entirely unjust criticisms which were leveled in many circles against the French episcopate before the Council. After the first session, however, it was universally conceded that the French bishops gave evidence of a tremendous concern for souls and of a deep and vital motivation of charity. Their love for the revealed truth was accompanied by a great respect for the Church and their fellow bishops. Indeed, here is a testimony which can have a tremendous influence for the good in the Church. A brisk exchange of ideas among the bishops of the various nations should prove similarly fruitful. It should have continuous good bearing on the care of souls and theology. Above all, it should be a powerful factor in safeguarding unity and promoting mutual love.

The Council will undoubtedly prove an effective spur to the permanent contacts of bishops in their relations with the universal Church on what we might call the horizontal level. However, without the stability which we hope to find in the episcopal conferences, these permanent contacts may not bear the rich spiritual fruit we desire.

The mission work of the universal Church, certainly supported primarily by the religious orders, clearly assures us of the horizontal contact between nations long Christianized and mission territories. In the Council likewise, the bishops of mission areas have something to offer; they contribute substantially to that form of renewal which places the catholicity of the Church more in evidence. We may well anticipate from the Council a second spring of missionary activity in which the roles of the episcopate, the episcopal conferences, and the individual dioceses could assume greater importance than they have had up to the present.

Over and beyond the mission task, the solidarity of the Episcopal College could look forward to a generosity that will balance the dioceses and nations suffering from a dearth of priests and those which are well supplied. Moreover, there could be an increase of mutual assistance in other areas, even in material aid. Though material bounty is not on the first level of missionary endeavor, it may not be discounted or undervalued, for it is also an expression of charity in the Church of the Word incarnate. The entire Church must cooperate in giving and receiving so that at all times and in all places she remains the Church of the poor.

Even in the apostolic and postapostolic Church there was bold discussion. Problems and sharp disputes about formulas were never absent. But the solution was always found in the churches and their respective bishops who remained in contact with one another on terms of love and mutual assistance. Modern means of communication facilitate such contacts. The present exchange of ideas on the international level and the existence of many flourishing international organizations and cultural forms outside the Church make it imperative today that we also have an international exchange of ideas and permanent mutual assistance in the episcopate. This is the command of the hour, the *kairos*.

The Roman Curia and the Episcopal College

The second comprehensive group of problems facing the Council concerns the functions of the Roman Curia in its relation to the Episcopal College.

The infallibility and the primacy of jurisdiction of the

pope as successor of St. Peter is a personal prerogative—a prerogative or privilege obviously to be understood in the sense of the *diakonīa*, which means work of service—belonging to the pope alone and not to the Curia. But the pope has need of a great staff of counselors and collaborators for the effective discharge of such an important office.

At this point we must ask what the structure of the Roman Curia should be if it is to strengthen in these times the unity of the College of Bishops and render most lovingly acceptable the function of the Bishop of Rome as head of the community of love in the entire Church. What are the relations between the universal episcopate and the Roman Curia, and what is the position of both confronting the successor of Peter? The questions present more than a fringe problem to the Council.

Dogmatically, there is no doubt that all the bishops of the earth are jointly and by ordinary right the counselors of the pope in all matters concerning the universal Church. This doctrine has nothing in common with the dated and condemned conciliar theory, which subjected the pope to the universal council, or with any false conception of the Church as a representative democracy—a false transfer of democratic concepts to the Church's constitution. It is simply the expression of the collegiate character of the episcopate under the successor of Peter. At the appropriate time and in full freedom the Supreme Pontiff gave solemn expression to this collegiality in the spirit of pastoral awareness when he convoked the Ecumenical Council. Whether or not this function of the College of Bishops can or must emerge with greater effectiveness in later times, after the

Council completes its work, is obviously for the Pope him-self to decide. What forms its activity will assume must like-wise be determined by the Pontiff himself. The Council will certainly not hesitate to take up the matter with him.

Modern means of communication make it very easy for any presiding bishop of an episcopal conference or for that matter for a delegate or any particular bishop chosen by the Pope to go to Rome at regular intervals for consultations. Singly or in groups they can be ready to act as counselors when called upon by the Holy Father. In this way the bishops would manifest and deepen the sense of solidarity of the universal episcopate and the entire Church with the successor of Peter as her head.

The College of Cardinals—progressively growing more international in the last few decades—now exercises a similar function. The cardinalate, however, is not of divine origin as is the episcopate. In consequence it can be exten-sively modified. In fact, it could theoretically be altogether abolished, though obviously no such thought has entered anyone's mind. In all this the right of the Pope to choose his own close collaborators and his right to enunciate defini-tive decisions on his own cognizance and with supreme authority are clear beyond doubt. The primacy of the Supreme Pontiff is a patrimony of faith solidly established. But certainly a development is possible in the direction of greater breadth and depth of solidarity in the College of Bishops.

If we assume that the universal episcopate is to cooperate more actively in the government of the Church throughout the world, we might likewise anticipate that the Roman

Curia might be relieved of certain tasks on the higher level. This release of responsibility of phases of authority would not derogate from the prestige of the Roman See; the immediate influence of the Pontiff and the universal esteem he enjoys, joined with the power of attraction the Roman Church has for the separated brethren, could result only in a notable increase of prestige for the papacy. Fundamentally this prestige of the Church and the Pope would surely be in the interest of the Curia itself, which has every reason to seek appreciation and honor throughout the whole Church for its exercise of unselfish service in testimony of love for the Church of Christ.

Without doubt there is a universal desire that the fundamental principle of Catholic social doctrine be made more effective in the organization of the Church. This is the principle of subsidiarity stressed strongly by Pius XI in the encyclical *Quadragesimo anno* and by Pope John XXIII in *Mater et magistra*. Many functions which in the course of centuries developed in centralized Roman officialdom can be entrusted to the bishops and patriarchs or the episcopal conferences. Such an organic return to the more ancient traditions would be an adjustment more fully in harmony with the needs of our times.

We should add that there is need for a much clearer distinction between the functions and tasks of Rome as patriarchal church of Italy and the West on the one hand and the supreme power of governing the entire Church on the other. After the great Eastern schism, the patriarchal functions and the universal primacy of the Bishop of Rome coincided concretely and practically since the Church had shrunk territorially. But today the Church embraces the whole world; she is more universal than ever before. Moreover, she plans to prepare herself by means of the most careful and precise measures for the readmission of the Christian communities separated from her. The great diversities in the one universal Church under the successor of Peter ought to be stressed anew.

As an organism expands, its functions must also be articulated and divided in accordance with its growth. In a religious order, to cite an example, the major part of the functions may be performed by the founder himself or by the superior general as long as the order is not extensive. But its gradual expansion demands progressive divisions into vicariates and provinces. And the provincial superiors are constantly given new tasks with extended powers or faculties, without any real jeopardy to unity. And because unity is retained, organic functioning is also retained without any loss of charity.

Restricted decentralization of functions according to the traditions of former ages would not at all result in a decline of influence in the center of Christianity. There are many kinds of spiritual and intellectual influence which need not and may not be exclusively or primarily administrative, nor need they be confined to the daily dispensing of favors or the issuing of directives. In the same direction of a more visible and more richly articulated unity is the desire of many of the fathers at the Council that the composition of the Roman Curia be international. The executive organs of the Pope in the Roman departments must as far as possible represent in an effective way the whole Catholic world—the experiences, the ways of thought, the feelings and preoccupations of the entire Church. If this goal is to be attained, the episcopate of all nations must show constant readiness to place at the disposal of the Pope priests who are fully suited to serve at the Curia. Above all, these priests must be expert in the care of souls, men whose presence would be a pledge of the pastoral spirit even in matters of administration.

Whereas the Catholic Church and the Pope of the Second Vatican Council have received singularly favorable reports from the world news agencies and journals, the judgments on the Roman Curia have often been quite the contrary, though they have frequently been unjust generalizations based on individual cases or episodes. Fortunately, there have been other voices and reports which have placed the conduct of the Curia in a more favorable light, as well they might, for the attitude and procedure of the great majority of cardinals and bishops of the Curia has been proper in every way.

It would seem that the Supreme Sacred Congregation of the Holy Office is the focal point of adverse criticism and misgivings in many quarters. World opinion, in a special manner that of the Christian communities not yet united to Rome, seems to share the view that the Holy Office is encumbered in its very structure with a heavy burden of historic liability, dating from the Inquisition, and that this liability has not yet been liquidated. This psychological difficulty must be dealt with and resolved with great charity and wisdom in order to secure unbounded confidence for the whole Roman Curia and welcome recognition of its service. Such acknowledgment is necessary not only in the Catholic world but also beyond, among all Christians who with sympathy turn to the Catholic Church.

The popes of the past century have enjoyed a truly universal esteem, and Pope John was extraordinarily esteemed and loved. But that the Pope is esteemed and loved is not enough if the instrument of his work, the Roman Curia, is in part discredited. Neither false impressions and illusions nor unsuitable anachronistic structures may be allowed to obscure the most exalted functions of the primacy of the Roman Bishop; nothing in the Church of Rome must cloud the union of love with the universal Church.

It is true that the Church of the Word incarnate requires juridical and administrative functions, but it is also necessary that every individual and every community examine their consciences about the manner in which they perform and fulfill these requirements. Are the exercise and administration of law and right totally expressions of charity? Do they really serve to edify the community of love? This period of the Council is the acceptable time for the entire Church to examine her conscience to see if the juridical and administrative institutions, as they have developed historically, serve to promote the community of love at the present hour. This examination of conscience demands abnegation and goodness on the part of all directed to all others. I say all, for we are not permitted to point an accusing finger at any single group as though they apart from all others are the black sheep.

Pope John clearly has created an atmosphere in which these tasks of the Council can be discharged with profit in a spirit of good will and absolute sincerity. From the very inception of his pontificate he honored and encouraged the bishops as his collaborators. Thus also he turned to his Curia in recognition, kindliness, and confidence. He assigned as the center of all the particular studies and discussions the great mystery of unity.

The cause of good would be jeopardized if in certain quarters false criticism were to be directed against the effort to create more adequate structures in the Church's administration. Great harm would be wrought if this reasonable desire for adjustments and modifications in the ecclesiastical machinery were interpreted as hypercriticism springing from selfish and opinionated minds. The whole Church is concerned. She sincerely probes her own conscience in the spirit of love. It is significant—we may consider it a symptom of what thoughts are stirring in men's minds, what emotions are rising in their hearts—that cardinals are expressing doubts about the *cappa magna* and similar pomp of church prelates: do these suitably manifest the Church of the poor with evangelical simplicity and a kingdom which is not of this world?

All things must be made to serve the community of love. All things must be turned to her use, presenting her as visible and attractive. In this community of love which is the Church, everything must redound to the praise and glory of the great mystery of love; the Church in all things must serve the mystery of love.

The assertions of Pope John and the official forms published by the Council give us reason to anticipate a clear doctrinal exposition, even though there may be no formal definition, of the collegiate character of the episcopate with the Pope at its head. This truth will be expressed even more clearly and concretely in the organizational structures and the laws of the Church. If in this way the interior unity of the Church is strengthened, her image in the minds and imaginations of men will be viewed in a more favorable light and in a sense be better understood by those outside the Church. Then we shall have a visible symbol, attractive to the Christianity which is separated from Rome, particularly to those groups which faithfully retained the episcopal constitution of the ancient Church or at least have newly discovered the significance of the episcopate and its collegiate character.

7

THE SANCTITY OF THE CLERGY

An ancient Oriental eucharistic prayer concludes with the refrain, "Fill our hearts with holiness; make us one in thy love!" Together the two petitions are basically nothing less than the carrying out of the priestly prayer of our Lord. At the Last Supper He begged of the Father first of all that in the apostolic College, in the Church's priesthood, the mystery of sanctity would be made visible through unity—"that they may be perfected in unity" (Jn 17,23). Every force working toward the sanctity of the clergy in the apostolic diffusion of their light, every impulse toward an increase of priestly vocations must tend to hasten the unity of the clergy, upholding it as the indispensable means to holiness as well as the most precious fruit of holiness.

Pope John also emphasized this particular phase of unity frequently. In a friendly address to members of the Apostolic Union of the Clergy, he stressed the point very effectively:

Among the universal cares of the supreme pontificate, it is a very great comfort to see the close unity and the wonderful harmony which the diocesan clergy manifest to us. As torches placed on a candelabrum, as a city built on a mountain, they are a pacific and generous force. By their example they edify souls and lend the splendor of radiant light to the sanctifying work of the Church. Our priests today as in all times sustain the loftiest ideals. They nourish the desire of a perfect sacerdotal life. They seek to strengthen the bonds of priestly fraternity in order that the spiritual and pastoral life of each one, the strict restraints of solitude having been surmounted, may develop with redoubled fervor and greater efficacy.[1]

On many other occasions he has pointed out how essential the bond of unity is for the sanctity of the clergy. Note the following: "Priests of Christ, we are immersed in the warmth which the fire of the Holy Spirit enkindles. We have received all from the Church. Let us therefore work in her name and under her authority; let us love to serve her in the bonds of unity and in that perfect manner with which she wills to be served."

Priests are not bound to the College of Bishops by purely juridical bonds. The bond between priest and priest and between priest and bishop is above all the indelible mark of priesthood with the redemptive love of the High Priest Christ Jesus resplendent in it. In the perfection of unity with their own bishop and in the College of Bishops through him, priests give testimony to the great mystery of unity. Priestly sanctity reveals itself in the unity which reflects that mystery. It prospers only in the atmosphere of truly priestly and pastoral fellowship.

Reviewing the history of the Church, we sometimes shudder over the ugly rivalry between the religious and the diocesan clergy, a rivalry which at times proved a serious

[1] *Discorsi, Messaggi, Colloqui del Santo Padre Giovanni XXIII*, I, 383.

obstacle to the whole work of the apostolate. The violent hostility, the distrust, and the work at cross purposes are probably things of the past, never to recur. Now we notice fruitful cooperation everywhere. The Council, however, is certainly in a position to make a contribution to this same collaboration, to the end that here the prayer of the Lord— "that they may be perfected in unity"—may be answered even more perfectly. Juridical structures and operations on the pastoral level in parish, diocese, and beyond and also in religious orders must be instruments to express the unity of all who are working for the care of souls, to gain them and shelter them.

Perhaps the privilege of exemption granted to religious orders should be submitted to a new study. New limitations and interpretations of the exemption, may be deemed necessary, but not a substantial reduction or a total suspension. Exemption in the last analysis serves the unity and universality of the pastoral service in the Church. Exemption is actually a privilege given by the Holy Father, for whom religious orders must hold themselves in constant readiness. It can and must be a safeguard of continuity and coherence in the care of souls, a continuity extending beyond the period of the individual bishop's reign and a coherence extending beyond the confines of a single diocese. Exemption indeed must always be understood in the sense that the religious clergy within the dioceses are a model in the common elaboration on a pastoral plane of a plan for the care of souls, a plan set up or at least approved by the bishop, and a model most particularly in the execution of that plan on a pastoral level.

Ignatius of Antioch, disciple of the apostles, considered the union of the clergy with the bishop in the light of the eucharistic experience. As the priests are gathered with their bishop around the altar in genuine concelebration, so in their unity they are essentially witness to the great mystery of unity and love. Not only the new liturgy but also the Church law (now being prepared) and the fundamental directives of pastoral endeavor must be above all a sign and witness of unity, must show plainly how the clergy are gathered in love, precisely in the unity of love, with the bishop as center.

In many dioceses the preparations for the Council produced as accessory fruit, though nonetheless precious indeed, a serious and open dialogue between the bishop and all the clergy, religious and secular, of the diocese, and at the same time a loving exchange of ideas between the laity and the bishop and priests. Such discussions undoubtedly have contributed to the elimination of uncharitable criticism and the increase of mutual confidence. They have provided a vehicle for priests to learn from one another through their contacts, thereby strengthening the bond of solidarity in the common striving for sanctity and the promotion of the apostolate.

Lively public discussions on the long-anticipated liturgical renewal, particularly of the breviary, have created in the minds of us priests the happy impression that the bishops consider themselves principally the spiritual fathers of their clergy. We can assume without fear of error that the common consultations in the Council have served to stress and confirm this disposition among the bishops.

What can the Council do, what will the Council do to strengthen and deepen the spiritual fellowship of priests with one another? The hope that at least under special circumstances they will be granted the privilege of true and complete concelebration of the eucharist with their bishop and also concelebration by those who work together intimately is only a part of this picture. Concelebration as an effective symbol of the mystery of faith and unity would create a deeper realization of the inner grace of fellowship.

Throughout the years of my priestly life I have had many associations with priests of all countries. From my contacts with priests, individually and in groups, I can establish that the more serious among them everywhere are quite conscious of the need for priestly fellowship. They spontaneously acknowledge how necessary it is for them to have mutually stimulating contacts with other priests in a common experience of true priestly unity.

8

The People of God

The First Vatican Council opened its dogmatic constitution on the Church with the stress on that unity which our Lord sought in His high priestly prayer. It is significant that the Council did not begin with the power of governing in taking up this point of the unity of the Church. The constitution begins with these words: "The Eternal Pastor and Bishop of our souls [an obvious reference to I Pt 2,25], in order to perpetuate the saving work of Redemption, willed to establish Holy Church in which as in the house of the living God all the faithful would be contained through the bond of one faith and charity." It then says in order that "the episcopacy be one and undivided" and that unity "of faith and communion" be preserved "through the priests united to one another," Peter was made the foundation and head of the Church.[1]

The Second Council of the Vatican, according to the pattern so clearly established by the Pope, will be able to make this introduction its point of departure when it takes up the doctrine on the laity, elaborating on the organic position in

[1] Denz. (32) 3050-51.

the Church of the layman and the organic membership of all baptized and all those who believe in Christ. In this connection the theology of the laity, immensely developed in the last several decades, may be recapitulated by the Council and brought to a fruitful conclusion. The Church, we hope, will profit greatly by this action.

The place of laymen in the Church cannot be explained primarily on a negative basis—they are not members of the clergy, do not belong to the religious state, and so on. Nor can it be explained on the basis of a condition of submission. The laity are active members of the people of God. They are accepted in the mystery of unity by service and by the testimony of the apostles and their successors. And together with the College of Bishops and the priests, they must render to the world testimony worthy of their faith in the great mystery of love, in humble and loving fellowship with the hierarchy and among themselves.

In his opening discourse, the Pope placed in starkest relief this function of the faithful. As already cited above, the Pontiff said that the Church through her sons extends the frontiers of charity everywhere, for charity removes dissension and promotes harmony, unity, and peace in the community of brotherhood.

It is well known that an appropriate commission concerned with the position of the laity in the Church was nominated by the Council. We do not doubt that the entire work of this conciliar commission and all the proposals in this area will be given their authentic direction by the great mystery of unity.

The layman is sanctified and made a member of the people of God through baptism. Baptism is the sacrament grafting the recipient to the Mystical Body of Christ, to the people of the New Alliance. This sacrament in a true sense makes all those our brethren who bear the name of Christ, even though they are not yet part of the visible community of the one Catholic Church. Baptism is the basis of our obligation to love and honor the separated brethren who through no personal fault have not yet found the true Church and to create in them, through a life of harmony with our baptism in fraternal union, a vivid realization that Christ has founded and commissioned the Church as the Father commissioned Him.

Confirmation, penance, and in a most singular manner the eucharist signify a progressively deepening penetration into the mystery of unity. Accompanying this is the sacred obligation to give testimony of this same mystery and to cooperate actively in the apostolate of the Church, whose end and purpose is the plenitude of unity in Christ and the conversion of all things in Christ and through Christ: "Instaurare omnia in Christo."

The liturgical renewal already approved by the Council in substance assigns to the layman a place which will render him more aware of his faith in the celebration of the sacred mysteries. From this vantage point he will also comprehend better the active role of his mission in the Church as a whole. "The layman in the Church cannot simply be he who hears and is silent, who permits himself to be moved but does not himself move or act. He should not be a stranger to anything which happens in the Church."[2] The reformed liturgy of itself will speak eloquently in its more accessible form and will lead to the mystery. For this very important reason, it must not simply be imposed upon the faithful or commanded. The faithful must be made capable through an interior motivation of contributing to this renewal. "Liturgical renewal without the participation of the faithful is impossible. And this participation must flow from a deeper understanding of the Christian mysteries and the true dimensions of common prayer. The Church is the community of those assembled by Christ—the community of those who are called together. The Greek word for Church indicates the call to assembly."[3]

A deepened comprehension and a more conscious and active fulfillment of the sacramental vocation according to the scriptural concept of "a kingdom of priests, a holy nation" (Ex 19,6) are the normal presuppositions for an active and sympathetic manifestation of a particular vocation in the layman.

The unity and health of an organism depend on every member's discharge of function. Each member must respond to his task. Only in case of necessity or emergency should a healthy member supply the functions another lacks. The effort, sometimes the predominant effort, to circumscribe the apostolate of laymen in the form of Cath-

[2] Émil Cardinal Léger, in *Informations Catholiques Internationales*, no. 171 (1962), p. 5.
[3] Émil Cardinal Léger, in *Responsabilités actuelles du Laïcat*, Montreal, 1961.

olic Action, which is understood as "participation with the hierarchical magisterium of the Church," overlooks the specific function of the layman as such. In consequence it overstresses the dependence of the lay apostolate on the directives of the hierarchy. Catholic Action in this sense is a noble auxiliary function of the laity in an area purely religious whenever the clergy is not adequate. Under certain historical circumstances, entirely unique or exceptional, Catholic Action could also constitute a common force guided by the hierarchy which would influence public life. In such an instance the specific competence of the laity would be accepted in a general plan for the Christianization of the environment.

A true and proper vocation of the layman, however, must be viewed in the light of his particular gifts of grace and of his position as witness to the faith. By a life according to the law of grace, he contributes to the inner fullness and unity of the Church. By his truly Christian life and his disinterested collaboration with all good men in his profession, in his leisure time, in cultural forms, in the orientation of public opinion, and in economic areas, the layman collaborates in the consecration of the world. He has a mission of his own in the world. It is strictly proper to the layman. He cannot accomplish it without being profoundly steeped in the truth and the life of the Gospel, being led thereto by the doctrinal and pastoral magisterium of the Church. But in the area of his competence he is not a functionary of the hierarchy. He manifests the Church, we might say he makes her present, in his life surroundings when he works under the influence of faith and in charity. Through the mature layman the Church becomes the vital principle of society.

Maturity of the layman in secular surroundings, maturity in the full Christian sense, naturally presupposes charity in humility and humble obedience in all that pertains to authority. But the spirit of humble obedience must characterize clergy as well as laity. There must be mutual service, service suited to each in his turn according to the spirit of Christ, Who became the servant of all. When the spirit of humility reigns in the Church, the spirit of mutual service for the good of all, then the way to the unity of the human race, according to the words of Pope John, is being prepared and consolidated. This unity forms the necessary foundation for the terrestrial city which is to be like the heavenly one "in which reigns truth, and charity is the law, and its boundary is eternity."[4]

The people of God—the Church—are still on pilgrimage with eyes turned to the heavenly Jerusalem. This hope and vigilance will preserve them from presumption and indolence. The people of God do not construct their dwelling place out of passing and transitory earthly things as though they were an ultimate end. But precisely in view of the redemption, the Church takes earthly things seriously. In Christ Jesus, in fact, God wills to turn all things to the reign of love, in which all men are brothers and sisters and all goods are gifts of God and instruments of fraternal love. To attain this ideal the people of God must engage in an ever-challenging struggle.

[4] St. Augustine, *Epist. 138, 3.*

Marriage and Family:
Community of Love and Salvation

The Council has been presented a schema on marriage and the family prepared by the theological commission. The official notices are not adequate to permit us to draw conclusions regarding the content and trends of the text. But at least from what has occurred thus far and from the discourse of the Holy Father at the first session, we can confidently hope that also in this area fruitful progress will be made along the lines of the sublime vision of John XXIII centering on the mystery of unity and love.

The family, according to an oft-quoted saying of St. John Chrysostom, is "a church in little," a union of cult, life, love, and salvation and a figure of the bond of love of Christ and the Church. Marriage today as perhaps never before in history is being attacked—by massive propaganda for birth control in order to keep the family artificially reduced, by a flood of divorces, and above all by a totally profane earthly vision, which is perhaps the deep root of all the evils. Christian spouses can resist these attacks only if they have grasped, and grasped vitally, the truth that only their sanctified love is the pure fountain of the fruitfulness willed by God. Once they arrive at a vital realization of the need for prayer and struggle, they can truly bear witness to the Christian meaning of marriage. Only through common prayer, sincere and persevering, and an earnest struggle to develop a conjugal love ever purer, ever stronger and more tender can they truly bear witness to the indissolubility of marriage and discharge their service toward life in the midst of a faithless and self-centered world.

Our teaching on the goals and purposes of marriage should not be placed in a mere biological framework concerned with the nature of the conjugal act. Nor should it be a marriage-ends doctrine directed toward the Aristotelian categories of end and means to end. Basically, these approaches do not come to grips with the meaning of conjugal love; they are not equal to the task involved in today's conflict with utilitarianism and sensualism. By contrast, the moral message of the Church can propose the entire marriage doctrine in the light of the great mystery of love. This message is directed to life itself in service, which means the penetration of life with absolute fidelity and the mutual responsibility of the spouses for each other's salvation. In this service there is a clear manifestation of the fertile and happy profundity of sacramental marriage. Those who are faithful to the light of this message more readily recognize the inconsistency and the peril of that love which fundamentally rejects this service to life and is premised on a loyalty revocable at the will of the parties. Much lauded today, this love cannot be harmonized with the Catholic moral message.

Moral imperatives alone and occasional hints regarding the couple's mutual responsibility for their eternal salvation do not communicate the Catholic message. Without the great communion of conjugal love, they will prove inadequate. If on the contrary everything is viewed under the aspect of the conjugal love of the spouses and this sanctified love in turn is contemplated in the light of the mystery of

salvation, of the trinitarian love of God, of the bond of
Christ's love for His Church, in its sublimity and profundity, in its breadth and depth, then indeed the charity of
Christ will embrace the conjugal love. It will move the love
of the spouses, the total conjugal love, to the fulfillment of
the command of grace of which the sacrament is the efficacious communication. Under this task of salvation are sub-
sumed all the moral commandments of marriage.

The sacramental dignity of Christian matrimony has
never been questioned in the Church. But the deeper meaning of the doctrine has not always been applied in a vitally
Christian structuring in religious formation for marriage. In
the face of the tendencies arising from a conception of marriage which is entirely profane and laicist, a comprehensive
concept of marriage as a sacrament has become urgently
necessary.

The dialogue with non-Catholic Christians demands of
us a more luminous, attractive, and profound presentation
of this truth. It must shun two extremes: it must both rise
above mere sacramentalism which is not vital and vigorous
and likewise transcend rigid moralism. Here, too, the discussion with others presupposes a humble reflection on ourselves.

The Catholic Church—this we stress regarding the attitude of Protestant Christians—has faithfully preserved the
true doctrine on the sacramentality of marriage. However,
legalistic tendencies and superficial moralism have largely
failed to display these treasures to the married. Often the
sacrament has been looked upon and explained exclusively
or at least primarily as a means of grace helping the Chris-

tian to fulfill a duty to which he is bound by law. Marital love, which through the power of the sacrament is a sanctified and sanctifying love, redeemed and redeeming, has often seemed to be alien to the sacramental point of view. Not rarely has love been imposed merely as a commandment and at the same time set forth in a way that almost implied it did not belong to the essence of matrimony. Sometimes it was more or less suspect as sentimentalism or, to speak more bluntly, as a simple urge, even though no one went so far as to agree with Kant in discarding it entirely as a pathological affair.

We are not to minimize or attenuate the traditional doctrine of the sacramentality of matrimony but rethink it, penetrate more deeply into it, and view it in its convincingly comprehensive structure with all its power to manifest its truth and meaning for the formation of life. Only in this way can we succeed in making the Catholic message acceptable also to the separated brethren. The ecumenical dialogue in this area will also enrich Catholic moral theology. It is rather obvious that a believing attitude directed to the word of God actually gives many Protestant Christians a better grasp of the nature of the mystery of Christian matrimony and the call of the married to true sanctity than have certain moral tracts written by Catholics. Many separated brethren have difficulty accepting the Catholic doctrine on marriage, though their problem is not so much in the doctrine as such; the stumbling block is rather the moralistic approach in its presentation. Marriage moralism as some present it seems to recognize only duty and to cast marriage solely in the light of purpose and end, paralleling a kind of

superficial sacramentalism—one as superficial as the other—
which is almost exclusively limited to conditions of validity
and the efficacious production of grace.

On the one hand the moral message of the Church must
build its defense against external errors, such as the notion
of artificial birth restriction which sanctions every arbitrary
intervention in the processes of life. On the other hand it
must be filled with profound compassion and manifest kind-
ness and sympathy for married couples who are entirely in
good faith but who are involved in difficulty with regard to
the manner of fulfilling the responsibility of parenthood.
Will the Council utter one clear word to them which safe-
guards the purity of their conjugal love and encourages
them to make an unflinching common effort? Will it distinguish without equivocation their sincere effort to im-
prove, to express more perfectly their love and their will to
respond generously to the demand for fecundity, from what
is characteristically conjugal onanism, an arbitrary decision
of will and a defective attitude toward serving the purposes
of life? According to the proceedings which we have followed up to now, and according to the very insistent words
of the Pope of the Council, we can confidently hope that
the Council will present the fundamental moral proposi-
tions in this area not as stones but as bread which truly
nourishes.

Another problem presses for consideration. The Second
Vatican Council cannot ignore the burning question of
mixed marriages. (We have in mind the marriage of two
baptized persons, one of whom is not a Catholic.) It would
perhaps be premature to predict what concrete directives

are to be given. Of one thing, however, we may be quite certain: we may confidently expect that all the questions in this area will be examined and discussed in the light of the mystery of unity. Christian marriage—and this includes mixed marriage—is to be understood as a union of grace in Jesus Christ. For this reason it is not lawful to enter into a mixed marriage if one party should endanger the salvation of the other. The Catholic party may not limit his concern to the matter of his own salvation, which signifies, among other things, that he cannot be entirely satisfied with the acceptance merely of the cautions by the non-Catholic party as demanded by ecclesiastic law. There is always the lurking doubt about the conscience of the other party: can the non-Catholic give the guarantees demanded in the cautions and still be in good faith? Can he still have a right conscience? The first and immediate concern of the Catholic party will not be to lead the other into the Catholic Church. Such a step would have to be completely rejected if it is apparent that it cannot be taken with true inner conviction. Nevertheless, the immediate expression of the union of grace will be the Catholic spouse's confirmation of the other in the common faith in Jesus Christ our Lord, in devotion and fidelity to the saving will of God. Thus, he will give testimony to a truly Catholic life of faith and charity. If then in God's grace the step to the Catholic Church is taken through inmost impulse, this will in no wise be the result of a proselytism inflicting violence on the other confession.

In one special way a new regulation in the law on mixed marriages insistently requested of the Council must bear witness to the great yearning of the Catholic Church for the

reunion of all Christians. The legislation on mixed marriage
formulated after the religious wars is in many points not
adapted to the present age, in which many who are not
Catholic join with us in invoking the name of Christ and
pray anxiously with us in St. Peter's for the return of unity.
With God's help, a way will be found which corresponds
both with the inmost demand of the convictions of Catholics everywhere and with our concern for the reunion of
all Christians.

9

The Social Message of the Church

The mystery of unity, according to the bold concept of John XXIII, is already operative in all men of good will, even if only incipiently. For this reason at least, the social message of the Church can be applied to all men. And this helps explain why the Catholic Church of the Second Vatican Council does not rest on earthly privileges and claims, whether inherited or acquired. The Church, as was clearly stated in the first message of the Council to the world, is conscious of her essential mission to mankind as a mission of service, and proposes her social message and her will to serve the greater good of the entire community of peoples according to that awareness.

The Gospel which the Church is commissioned to proclaim today as from the beginning is neither first nor last an earthly social doctrine. Also, in the Second Vatican Council the Church places first the kingdom which is not of this world (Jn 18,36). The great mystery of unity is a reality of the other world, which is nevertheless already operative through grace in the present world of space and time. The kingdom of the other world is a far cry from the Marxian expectation of redemption as a future ultimate reign in peace flowing from human struggles and wars. The mystery of unity is already present in our world through the incarnation, which in an incomprehensibly real and vital manner affects all areas of our life. So exalted is this mystery that it must radiate light and warmth on all men, whatever their race or social position.

With singular insistence the Church of the Second Vatican Council must create a true consciousness among men, a consciousness of the Church as a handmaiden who is at the service of all. In this way men of the most diverse backgrounds and cultures will hearken with confidence to the Church's social message; the result should be that the proclamation of the rights of God, sovereign in His love for all men, will become credible and acceptable to all.

In fulfillment of its exalted mission in all ages, the Universal Council provided the human spirit with security in the acceptance of the faith by making use of all the intellectual instruments of the times to attain its goal. The present Council seeks this same goal with even greater urgency; in harmony with the express intent of Pope John, it must promote the renewal of the Church in the spirit of the Gospel. Accordingly, the Church of the Council must herself open her heart to the word of God with renewed vigor, and at the same time probe the intellectual currents of today's world to their depth; her purpose is to bear her ancient message to the world of today in a manner in which it can understand: "Hence, if the Council is to succeed, it is fundamentally necessary to probe the intellectual world of today with anxious care. We wish to set up anew the lamp of the Gospel, so that its light is not placed under a bushel of ancient forms but in the clear view of all who live in our presence!"[1]

The social message of the Church of the Second Vatican Council cannot be made acceptable to the twentieth-century mind if it is presented in the garb of the so-called European Christian culture. In any such presentation the cultural association would obscure the absolute and transcendent quality of Christianity in the minds of all those men of good will who question the validity of Western culture. The culture of the West with its origin and development in the Christian setting has become increasingly suspect to these men. Becoming more questionable day by day, this culture reflects discredit on Christianity through all too close association. In the vivid impression created by the unspeakable cruelty of two world wars, for which responsibility rests above all on peoples reputedly Christian, the myth of the superiority of Western culture over all others is definitely exploded. In reality it was never sincerely and openly Christian. Many elements of the ancient pagan world—Greek, Roman, Celtic, German—were grafted onto it without having been thoroughly Christianized. Moreover, the transition from a basically clerical culture to the secular culture of the present Western world did not follow a consistently organic and orderly process. It took place in a broad climate and atmosphere of bitter struggle; war, offensive and defensive, of the laity against a clergy entrenched in privilege

[1] Joseph Cardinal Frings, conference at Genoa, November 20, 1961, in M. Gozzini, *Concilio Aperto*, Florence, 1962, p. 32.

led unavoidably to war against the Church and Christianity.

Confronted as never before by European culture and Christianity, the peoples of Asia and Africa are scarcely aware of these historical complexities. In consequence they would be all the more inclined to hold Christianity accountable for the negative elements of modern Western culture the more the Church, and particularly her social message, is presented to them in close association with this same culture. Even the modern European or American is not deeply impressed by a presentation of the Christian message in the trappings of Western Christian culture. Christian social doctrine in the garb of an epoch in decline cannot attract him, even though it is proposed as distinct from Christian dogma. He would not look upon the Christian social message as offering an essentially dynamic structure for a new social order. Neither East nor West today finds in Western culture an approach to the transcendental and absolute in Christianity, an accessory motive of credibility.

The emergence of new worldwide perspectives has disillusioned the man of the West. It has made him conscious of the limits of his cultural and historic significance. As a result, one of the most important external supports of his faith in the absolute superiority of Christianity has been taken from him. He is now delivered over to the relativism which characterizes almost the whole of the current intellectual and spiritual life. Widely and subtly, this relativism extends its influence, not even sparing the ranks of the faithful. Let us not deceive ourselves: relativism is not necessarily a total or unmixed evil. If it should clear the atmosphere for a realistic perception of the relativity of all human cultural structures and forms and create in all parties a modesty of judgment toward one another, it would contribute mightily to better understanding among men. If relativism produces in us the modest judgment that our own human-historical heritage is not absolute, then it can help bring about a new understanding among men and open boundaries hitherto sealed. If relativism serves to create an understanding of the relative in mere human forms and structures, in virtue of which they are transient and mutable, it can contribute toward the removal of the barnacles of the sham absolute, presenting the real more clearly in its objective dignity and authenticity.[2]

There is a parable for us today in the call of Abraham. As Abraham had to abandon his homeland and his own people in order to build the future promised him, so the Church today is called to divest herself of her Occidental past and assume a position of service on a worldwide scale. In the present historic moment of the Second Vatican Council, the Church must again become the servant of all in virtue of her very catholicity: she must become the handmaiden of all mankind. Certainly she may not disown what is good and valid in the culture of the West, for she must continue to use it and work in its setting. But without embarrassment or prejudice she must recognize what is of worth and value, what is admirable in other cultures. She must address her message to all people of all cultures in order to shape the destiny of the whole human family. For the very reason that it is catholic, universal, her message must rise above every individual culture in order to be effective in every cultural form.

In principle these perspectives are universally recognized

[2] Ibid.

in the Church today, thanks in great part to the great predecessor of John XXIII. In the messages of Pius XII our doctrine is placed on a solid foundation. But to draw the conclusions of the doctrine, to point out the practical consequences of the theory—despite the truth and validity of these perspectives—is not easy, precisely because we are so thoroughly conditioned by our own culture. With heart and mind we are too much bound up in the culture of the West. In consequence, an enormous task confronts us, an urgent task to which we have scarcely set our hands. We must loosen the perennial and eternal in the Church's teaching from the transient and temporal with which it is vested, from the European idiom, from ecclesiastic procedure, in order to discover in the unity and diversity of forms new modes of expression accessible to the whole modern world. From the Council itself we should anticipate vigorous encouragement of renovation and the clear enunciation of principles with some model guidelines for their practical application. Of special value will be the wisdom of the bishops and theologians of other cultures whose voices are now raised so insistently for the first time at an ecumenical council.

The Church also lives in a pluralistic society in her European-American environment, in which she must clearly bear witness to her unique message of salvation. She must testify that she does not consider one religion as good as another in this unique essential. But on the level of natural knowledge and wisdom, she can enter—particularly through her lay sons—into fruitful dialogue with the followers of

other religions and of secular philosophies. One instance of
such cooperation relates to love and social justice particularly in their concrete application at an historic moment.
More than at any previous age in history the parable regarding the spoils of Egypt, used by the Fathers of the
Church in earliest Christian times, is valid today. They
spoke very significantly of the spoils of Egypt as a symbol
of the intellectual treasure of Greek learning taken over by
Christian thinkers to enrich Christian thought.[3]

The Church is not at all a monopolistic society in her
relation to culture and the social formation of life. There
are many areas in which she has no dogmas to offer. On a
thousand questions in the area of sound public opinion the
Church can exercise an influence through her open dialogue
with all men of good will. And the greater the openness of
her dialogue, the greater will be the value and worth of her
influence. Should she, however, approach the modern world
insisting on an uncritical acceptance of her attitudes toward
the multiple problems in the social structuring and forming
of life, the very definition of which is subject to historic
facts and realities, then indeed she would incite against herself reactions similar to those provoked by monopolistic
societies.

Not all the initiatives to good in the modern world flow
from the Church. Whatever it be, wherever it be, the
Church has every reason to rejoice in every good work and

[3] [The biblical reference is to Ex 12,35 f.; before their departure
from Egypt, the Hebrews obtained from the Egyptians articles of
gold and silver and clothing, thus despoiling the Egyptians and enriching themselves.—Tr.]

remain completely tranquil regarding its source. Such acknowledgment is in praise of the Giver of every gift, in praise of the mystery of unity in some way effective in all that is good.

From the days of controversy over membership in neutral trade unions on the part of some Catholics who felt they were obliged to condemn outright as reprehensible inter-confessionalism every species of cooperation with Christians of other confessions, even in merely civil or social matters, to the Second Vatican Council, much, very much has happened. But how much further in this direction can the people of God still go? How much further must they still go? The inquiry is entirely in conformity with the guiding ideas of the Council.

In recent years the Church has repeatedly stated her conviction regarding two groups of problems which absolutely demand friendly cooperation among all men of good will. Her stress of the need for the widest possible collaboration has found universal acceptance. In his *Mater et Magistra* and elsewhere, John XXIII placed the center of gravity in the Church's social message to the world today in the solidarity of all peoples in the universal struggle against human misery and social injustice. His message was widely accepted beyond the confines of the Church, and the Council fixed its attention on this point in its first message to the world. The Church can reveal her true countenance to the world as the Church of the poor in this historic hour only if Catholics, as a community and as individuals, proceed with great magnanimity and cooperate in the most effective way with all men of good will. Their concern is with the first great problem: the struggle against hunger.

Cooperation in this ideal of the Pontiff is evident, if we may cite one illustrious example, in the action of the German episcopate. Though their work is only a beginning, they have provided immediate help in many social necessities, above all by turning the tide of public opinion in favor of decisive help for undeveloped regions on the part of richer countries. This concrete and practical beginning of collaboration calls for a clear-cut statement from the Council, because we are still very far from a solution of the problem.

The other problem is the work for peace, as indicated in the recent encyclical *Pacem in terris*. Though the Church has always proclaimed a peace which is not of this world, the messianic salvation stands in the strictest relation to the sacred obligation of the human family to live in peace, and the Church is always the servant, the handmaiden, of the glad tidings which bring to men peace on earth.

Anyone who is dedicated to the great mystery of unity and its manifestation in the center of history is obliged to do all in his power to banish wars among the peoples of the one family of God. With the grace of God, the Council is confident that it can offer the world of today, which lives in fear, better ways to peace, ways more secure in that they are not ways of destruction depending on arsenals of atomic arms and the menace of their destructive power. The message of peace from the Council must be as concrete and specific as possible. Perhaps it will be possible to establish immediate contact with all Christian communities on this level. In fact, the effort should be made to establish contact with all religions, Christian and non-Christian. In this way, God willing, we may be able to pave the way toward collaboration with all men; our hope is a future in peace.

III

THE CONVERSION OF
ALL CHRISTIANS TO UNITY

In the Gospel parable of the prodigal son, the elder brother does not play a minor role. The younger brother who left the paternal roof to seek his pleasures in the world is sincerely repentant and returns home in all humility. He is singularly fortunate to have been accepted again, by his father's act of pure grace. But the elder brother, in his presumed righteousness, does not even deign to enter his father's house where a festive banquet has been prepared for the "good-for-nothing" younger brother. The parable is a lesson on smugness and self-righteousness; it is a pointed criticism of the self-righteous in the synagogue, of those who are just according to the law, of those of whom the Lord says in another Gospel passage that they themselves will not enter into the kingdom of God and they will not allow others to enter who seek to enter the kingdom (see Mt 23,13).

The Church as such will never become a self-righteous and unfaithful synagogue. She is the people of the Covenant of the new and eternal Testament, the chosen people to whom the Lord has bequeathed the kingdom. But she is never certain that her loyalty will be perfect; she must lament her shortcomings, her partial failure to measure up to her own ideals, and must constantly struggle to perfect her loyalty. Temptation constantly assails her in her individual and community members through the spirit of self-satisfaction and justice according to the law.

Was it not also to a shocking degree the lack of the spirit of penance in the Catholic Church, the lack of humble and loving sympathy, which led to the great schism of the East? Was the schism not at least partially owing to the haughtiness of the Latins, who sought to impose their own cast of thought in theology and cult on the Eastern brethren as the condition for their reacceptance into the Church?—and all this often despite express conciliar and papal attitudes and explanations acceptable to both sides? Do not Catholics share the blame for the exodus of many of the reform-minded circles from the Church in the Reformation period? We need not speak of the licentiousness and the moral decay, but was there not also the presumption of right and justice according to the law on the part of Catholics?

Joyfully we return thanks to God that today so many of the separated brethren refuse to make a case against the Catholic Church. They probe their own consciences. They also ask themselves in the presence of Peter, who spoke through the lips of the kindly John, "Brethren, what shall we do?" They heed the summons to do penance and return home. They direct our attention to the noblest Catholic heritage when they consider the whole Christian life as a continuous conversion and apply this doctrine also to their Christian communities. For those who are in the Church the situation presents a new and grace-laden motive for re-considering many points on their part. All the measures and guidelines of John XXIII constantly converge on this ad-monition: we Catholics must correct many errors affecting our attitudes in order that Catholic truth in its entirety may be made more acceptable to our separated brethren.

10

The Need for Renewal
Within the Church

Without doubt, the Catholic Church has preserved intact
the sevenfold sacramental system. But the Western Church
is now in a stage of serious rethinking, and humbly acknowl-
edges the need for a profound renewal in the celebration of
the sacred mysteries. We learn from the Eastern Church,
and in the last analysis this means from the best Catholic
tradition, that it is not sufficient merely to observe the
rubrics in the celebration of the liturgy. The sacred sign
must lead to the mystery, and the worship in its totality
must be the fundamental pattern and norm of our life,
which derives its force from the fountain of the sacred
mysteries.

Surely the Catholic Church has preserved revealed truth
from every formal error, at least as far as the actual dogmas
of faith are concerned. But have we not frequently entered
into violent debate over abstract truth? We need only think
of the unbelievable calumnies leveled against our best
exegetes by fanatics who did not take the trouble to under-
take thorough biblical study but nonetheless indulged in

the luxury of critical judgments. We need only recall the controversies, for example, over the problem of sufficient (and efficacious) grace and divine foreknowledge. We need only think of the unfortunate quarrel about ritual forms in which pseudodogmatic arguments were advanced to impose Western forms on the Asiatic world.

Have we not now and then presented Catholic truth to our separated brethren in the form of a stone rather than as well-prepared and truly nourishing bread? Have we always discerned their real needs, even hidden in their errors?

Not rarely in Catholic circles the scholastic method has been looked upon in a very narrow and falsely understood sense as the one certain method. For the sake of this presumed assurance, there was a renunciation of other methods of presentation. We failed to present our glorious truth in a manner which was acceptable also to others. And what is worse, in some circles those theologians who attempted to do this very thing were superficially dismissed as suspect.

Surely we have studied Moses and the Law and we have also rigorously defended the Law and natural right! All this is beyond question! But in the presentation of moral doctrine in Catholic texts and likewise in the practical procedures of the care of souls, we have often failed to stress the law of the Spirit. We must again be reminded of the words of St. Paul: "For the law of the Spirit of the life in Christ Jesus has delivered me from the law of sin and death" (Rom 8,2). Often the Christian has been introduced onesidedly to an external obedience, simply for-

malistic, instead of being led to the liberty of the sons of
God in a loving and generous obedience to the law of grace
and the Spirit with correspondingly vitalized obedience to
the external law.

The Second Vatican Council, inaugurated by the opening discourse of John XXIII, promises to become an open
confession of the Church that she stands in need of the
spirit of penance. She desires to divest herself of all legal
harshness and of all dead formalism to enter into the most
intimate union with revealed truth and with the great commandment of love. This done, she hopes to be able more
humbly and more efficaciously to invite the separated
brethren to return. Among the fathers of the Council there
is evidence of an ever-present determination to ponder, to
rethink, and wherever there may be need for it to reform
all that is purely of human tradition. We say human tradition, for there is surely to be no rethinking in the sense of
infringement of eternal truth or moral principles by way of
concession to human frailty. But there will be a more faithful and forthright grasp and appreciation of the truth of the
Gospel and of those sublime norms of Christian life which
we embrace and celebrate in the sacred mysteries.

The fathers of the Council will not rest satisfied with the
present attitudes and dispositions for penance and the trans-
formation of Christian life. New perspectives loom up before them at every new turn of events. They are concerned
with obedience to the Holy Spirit and His superabundant
gifts. We can hope for great things, the fruit of the profound patience, mortification, and prayer of the faithful.
The forces at work in the Council for a renewal are sus-

tained by an inner disposition and readiness for penance and reformation on the part of the entire believing world. The fact that the pastors of the Church go about the great task confidently imposes upon all, priests and laity, the obligation to second their efforts and to open up new perspectives before them through more intense prayer and a more profound penitential spirit.

No one in this time of grace can be so presumptuous as to pretend that he does not stand in need of a deepening of his own conversion. We may not even assume there is no such necessity even in the community of the entire Church in her external manifestation. The Church who invites the separated brethren, the Church of penitents, is not permitted to indulge in self-righteousness. She prays daily over the entire earth with greater ardor than ever: "Forgive us our trespasses!" Hence, she is less likely to be confused with the elder brother in proportion to the promptness and humility with which she opens her heart to the younger brother—that is, to the Christian communities separated from her—preceding him in the spirit of penance and confessing, "Father, I have sinned!"

To apologize for things of the Church which do not correspond fully with the truth darkens the testimony the Church must always render to unimpeachable truth. Self-defense, even when it is in accord with historic facts (though not with the demands of charity and of the present apostolate), does not measure up to the full dignity of the truth, the image of Him Who, being Truth, breathes Love. The use of truth patterned after the divine image must always be accompanied by an awareness of service in the interests of unity. Thus, the full truth is served in the light and warmth of love.

A self-defense which in any way savors of self-justification and constantly demands new and repeated rebukes and reproaches psychologically provokes countercharges and self-defense on the part of others. It follows a special pattern of deadly legality in the solidarity of the sons of Adam in evil.

Certainly, as informed and sympathetic children of the Church we will defend her against her enemies and against any hostile calumny. But are we not often too hasty to denounce as enemies, if they do not understand us perfectly, those who deep down in their hearts desire nothing more than to embrace us wholeheartedly as brothers? And do we not assume at times postures of defense or rush to a counter-attack when in reality others have shown a real need and we, to admit the truth, have made the path of unity difficult for them without any real necessity to do so?

Noblesse oblige. Humble acknowledgment of truth without any mixture of recrimination and self-defense opens the heart of man to the full truth, particularly if it is joyfully announced, and awakens in others the disposition of humility and frankness. Nor does this fall entirely within the limits of the reaction measured by our known laws of psychology; in the ultimate analysis we are dealing with the solidarity of salvation in Christ. With the flint of self-justification we cannot enkindle the flame of charity.

That the spirit of penance in the Catholic Church is the

noblest gift to the separated brethren can also be deduced from the statement of the noted Protestant theologian and observer at the Council, Oscar Cullmann:

When we return to our homeland and speak to the members of our churches on the renewal which we await from the Council, we must be very careful to warn our fellow believers, Protestant and Orthodox, against assuming a certain pharisaical posture as though our churches do not have need to reform themselves continually in the Holy Spirit according to the light of the Bible. We must in fact ask ourselves whether or not on certain points instead of a concentration we have introduced a limitation and restriction in the light of the Bible. Perhaps our churches have failed in permitting certain biblical elements to be slighted or lost.

11

THE MYSTERY OF UNITY
AMONG OUR SEPARATED BRETHREN

A more perfect and more convincing unity of Catholics among themselves, which must be maintained in exemplary solidarity, is a goal in itself; it is directed to the praise and glory of the trinitarian love of God and to the salvation of the Christian people. This unity, however, seems to be, at least in some degree and according to the ordinary ways of divine providence, a basic necessity and presupposition for the reunion of all Christians in the bosom of the Church. Every force for more intimate and more efficacious unity in the Church turns to the high priestly prayer, "that the world may know that thou hast sent me, and that thou hast loved them even as thou hast loved me" (Jn 17,23). The fulfillment of the great commandment in the bosom of the Church, her testimony to the great mystery and commandment of love, luminous and visible also to those far off—these are above all an invitation to those Christian communities still separated from her. All Christian men, however, must consider themselves obliged to pray for this ideal and strive to realize it. With all their power they should pray and strive for the re-establishment of unity in love and unity in faith so that they will be able to discharge faithfully the duty of their mission to the non-Christian world.

Since the very inception of John XXIII's pontificate, the concern evidently dearest to his heart was the reunion of Christians. But he did not view this from the standpoint of man's action or the course of human events. He saw rather in the spirit of faith how the great mystery of unity, the triune love of God, the grace of the Holy Spirit, is already at work everywhere. As a good gardener, he saw first the seed breaking through the soil, then the delicate plant, and then buds promising blossoms and fruit. All this he saw as the fruit of the Lord's prayer for unity. The most insistent motive for unbroken service in the re-establishment of perfect unity is the charity of Christ everywhere pressing, everywhere effective. In this vision we understand the Pope's words in the opening discourse of the Council.

The Catholic Church considers it her duty to strive earnestly for the fulfillment of the great mystery of that unity for which Christ Jesus prayed so ardently to His heavenly Father on the eve of His sacrifice. The realization that she is connected so intimately with this, creates ineffable sweetness of peace and joy in the Church. Should she not rejoice sincerely when she sees this prayer produce the most abundant and salutary fruits even among those who are outside her fold?

The words of Pope John were more than a mere gesture of courtesy toward the Christian communities outside the Catholic Church, which with such exemplary charity offered public prayers for the success of the Council. They were above all a loving return of thanks and still more a moving act of praise for the work of divine grace when the Pope said that unity spreads its light also in the unity in prayer and in the ardent desire with which the Christians separated from this Apostolic See yearn to be united with us.

John, the Pope, whose paternal heart was open to all, as he himself stated in his allocutions, saw the mystery of unity already operative in the esteem and respect toward the Catholic Church shown by those who belong to religions which are not Christian. From the following words it is clear that precisely this believing confidence reveals the work of God's grace effectively everywhere. In a most efficacious way, grace inflames the desire always to do something greater for the realization of perfect unity, so that all may be perfected in the unity of praise and glory of God, one and triune: "It is sad indeed . . . that an immense portion of the human race—even though no one is born on this earth who is not also redeemed by the blood of Christ—does not share the sources of supernatural grace which are in the Catholic Church."

If we understand the signs of the times and if we hearken to the voice of the Supreme Pastor of the Church with faith, we shall be disposed to re-examine our inmost thoughts. Every word of ours, every deed and our whole conduct, must be re-examined in order to see if we are in agreement in all things with the great design of our divine Master, "that they all may be one."

The Separated Christians in St. Peter's Basilica

The Second Council of the Vatican is not a council of reunion, nor does it assume to be such, in any direct or immediate sense. In fact, it renders a tremendous service to the unity of Christianity by avoiding direct discussion of reunion. The simple reason is that the time is not ripe for such discussion or for reunion itself. For this reason and not because of lack of motivation, the Council prefers that in the very heart of the Church and before all mankind there be an examination of conscience on the mystery of unity in the light of the mystery of love. Are we ourselves inwardly really ready to receive and welcome the brethren; are we prepared for a fruitful dialogue? For the very cause of unity, which we all crave, the Council seeks to be a council of renewal.

By way of caution, we must point out that interior renewal is not simply a means of paving the way for fruitful discussions with those who are not Catholic. A renewal of this kind in the Church is a grace and a work proceeding from the mystery of the love of God present in her. Her own vocation presses the Church to enter into herself in profound contemplation. Her inner unity must be more radiant; mutual love and understanding among Catholics of the most diverse schools, cultures, and nations must increase. The diversity of forms manifesting her will to serve in the spirit of a more loving unity must be more clearly recognized and appreciated.

The very impressiveness of the Church's action is a preparation for unity. The obvious fact that she has initiated what is properly called a serious wrestling with the issues, that she has made painstaking efforts and offers prayers for renewal, and that she has undertaken the restoration of unity within Christianity herself with the repentant spirit of confession before God, all of this is an initial fulfillment

of the exhortation of the apostle, "Confess, therefore, your
sins to one another, and pray for one another, that you may
be saved" (Jas. 5,16). The discussions are frank, and even
though they concern the most intimate matters of renewal
in the Church, they are not held in secret. The observers are
invited to all sessions, in spite of the serious misgivings of
some influential men who objected to the presence of non-
Catholics at discussions which would unavoidably involve
the clash of the divergent opinions within the Church herself. Did they in the ultimate analysis have some reason to
conceal from others our own admission of insufficiency, of
defects and sins? Or did they perhaps fear that the presence
of Eastern or Reform Christianity would embarrass the
bishops and put a brake on their frankness and courage in
effecting indispensable reforms in the very bosom of Catholicism?

Happily, the result was quite the contrary. The Catholic
Church is readying its own house and is determined to put
it in order in such a way that the others, those who are
without, can more easily recognize and more willingly
acknowledge that it is their own house, according to the
first pastoral address of John XXIII in words directed to
them: "They do not find a strange and alien dwelling,
but their own house, precisely that which their own venerable fathers from immemorable times have illumined with
their teaching and adorned with their virtue."[1]

The presence of the observers at the Council in the
Basilica of St. Peter is a near-miracle, revealing an astonishing change of attitude in both parties. The Church

[1] Pope John XXIII, radio message of October 30, 1958.

obviously invited the observers not to repeat the ancient anathemas against them but to have them as witnesses of her confession of penance and great concern for inner renewal, which is a gift of the Holy Spirit. No less astonishing is the fact that nearly all non-Catholic groups have sent observers.

In the course of the first session of the Council, the observers and separated brethren have become in common prayer and mutual effort *dilecti fratres observatores, carissimi fratres*—beloved observer brothers, most dear brethren. Though they do not enjoy actual conciliar membership and a vote with the fathers of the Council, they nevertheless make their presence felt at the Council in a unique way. Professor Cullmann, who comprehensively expresses the sentiments and impressions of all the observers, made this point very plain in his statement to the press on November 23, 1962.

Our presence—I agree entirely in this matter with what Cardinal Bea has said about it—is really a miracle. When I look about every morning at the places we occupy, places of honor facing the cardinals, when the secretary of the Council proclaims the *exeant omnes* [let all depart] every morning, while we remain in our places, I consider the manner and mode with which we are welcomed at this Council a never-ending marvel. I agree with Cardinal Bea that it is a near-miracle, above all when I call to mind what Councils have meant in the past for Christians who are not Catholics. I do not know if all the laity clearly realize the full meaning of our presence here from this point of view.

The "most dear brethren" are not merely passive onlookers. They are discernibly and effectively brothers. I recall the reaction of a Protestant theologian who some years ago was present at a meeting of various religious groups. After the meeting he said to me, with tears in his eyes, "Even if we cannot yet call one another brothers without restriction, we are still more than mere stepbrothers." This brotherhood, in the new light of recent events, sees union founded on baptism in the name of the one same and common Lord Jesus Christ, in the common treasure of truth, piety, and Christian formation of life. It is the expression of the fatherly love of Christ, who through His Holy Spirit works everywhere and in all. It is, however, a common fellowship in suffering patiently the trial of separation. And it is more, for it is a sympathy in mutual suffering and a sharing of mutual joy. Again Oscar Cullmann made this point very clear:

Our intimate participation in the acts of this Council presents to my way of thinking an important realization, a stage, really, of ecumenical thinking. Though externally we are passive observers, internally we vitally experience these proceedings with our Catholic brothers. Following the proceedings we take the same positions interiorly as do the Catholic participants, either for or against. This has truly brought us closer together in a very special manner during these recent weeks.

The participation of the brother observers involves something more than a mere interior sharing of experience in the conciliar discussions. *The observers are also heard.* The Secretariat for Christian Unity considers their wishes and brings them to the attention of the Council. Not rarely their thought is truly Catholic. Many of the bishops of the Council are engaged in a very intense exchange of views with them. Prejudices on both sides disappear.

12

Toward a More Fruitful Catholicity

The amicable presence of the observers is an accessory motive which should not be underrated psychologically and which obliges the fathers of the Council in a very special manner to formulate their utterances and their votes with Catholic breadth and precision. There is no place at the Council for mere scholastic theories and controversies. The Eastern and Reform brethren who listen to the discussions want to know precisely what is Catholic doctrine and what is not. Beyond this, they anticipate—and the point is particularly significant—a formulation which is accessible to all. With few exceptions, the language of the Council is Latin. But this is no mere synod of the Latin Church. Oriental theology communicates with fluency and ease. Patristic and even more so biblical thought must also feel at ease in the Vatican Basilica. How could we fail to make this truly Catholic mode of thought and language our vehicle of communication when we have invited guests who follow this type of speech—even though it may be in what we often call Church Latin—more readily than an exclusively neoscholastic formulation?

The Church of the Council seeks to be heard by the present-day world. Her word is spoken by believers who live and think and must bear witness to their faith in this same world of today. For this reason the Church of the Council must be as realistic as possible. She can venture forth toward this goal and hope to attain it only if she hearkens in faith to the word of God received from sacred Scriptures. In its daily enthroning of the Book of books at the opening of the sessions, the Council testifies that it stands in the shadow of the word of God and is able to penetrate the age with it only by heeding its teaching obediently. This twofold attention to the word of God, that of the word of the Bible and that prepared by God in the *kairos*, the summons of the age, unites us in a truly Catholic manner with all Christians. Thus is manifested to ourselves and to the observers the bond between sacred Scripture and living tradition. The greater the reverence we manifest for the rich heritage of past ages, in which the ancestors of the separated brethren still lived together with ours in the one house of the Church, the more Catholic we are and the more fruitful will be our dialogue with the separated brethren.

A certain integralism is found in some quarters today. It is the result of a grave apprehension for the purity and integrity of the faith, manifested whenever human traditions in the Church are challenged. We notice this misgiving in every area of change—from the revision of the law of eucharistic fast to the movement in favor of concelebration and the granting of the chalice to the laity.

Could we not reply to this earnest criticism that men's

faith should deepen when in the light of renewal they learn to distinguish more clearly the divine tradition in the Church from the human? The signs of the times indicate the need for a Christian maturity and adulthood. Only one who is able to distinguish between the immutable heritage of the faith and the time-conditioned laws and forms of piety can venture into the encounter with the world of today as a lay apostle.

But the capacity to make these distinctions is also demanded by the very inner nature of Catholicity itself. When Catholics align themselves with the contingent or temporal and think they are obliged to accept contingent theological doctrines which are not at all the final utterance of theology as truth infallibly proposed by faith, then in themselves and in their testimony they restrict the dimensions of that glorious Catholicity of the Church which the Apostle to the Gentiles expressed in the following manner: "Therefore let no one take pride in men. For all things are yours, whether Paul, or Apollos, or Cephas; or the world, or life, or death; or things present, or things to come—all are yours, and you are Christ's, and Christ is God's" (I Cor 3,21-23).

An unreflecting loyalty to yesterday and the day before yesterday, a blind opposition to the valid Pauline attitude of the reformed, to the Johannine-sacramental vision of the East, narrows one's own Catholicity. It means not to submit to Christ with that generosity which Jesus wills in drawing all things to Himself. Paul and John belong to the Catholic Church as truly and as exactly as does Peter.

Catholicity demands humility on the part of all Catholics. Catholicity is not reflected in fixed and static perfection in one theological school, or one parish, one diocese, one rite, or even one head and one heart. The image of Christ shines forth only from the diversity of the gifts of grace, in the rich prism of the saints of all epochs and all places. Catholicity presses toward development.

Regarding moral teaching, let us investigate a situation with which I am well acquainted in my capacity as a moralist: not one of the books of Catholic moral theology of the last few centuries usually looked upon as classical texts in this field presents to us and even less to our separated brethren so much as a bare notion of the wealth and the beauty of Catholic moral doctrine. We could not even be satisfied with ourselves in the sense of being able to say we have done our very best and have incessantly begged to obtain the gift of presenting in the most convincing manner in all its vast dimensions the length and breadth, the height and depth of the morality of the Christian life. We must rather acknowledge that we have not even been truly aware of our inadequacy. Those who now and then adverted to the insufficiency of the moral texts and expressed their profound regret about it were regarded by many as somewhat lacking in Catholic loyalty.

What does the Council ask of moral theology in view of the presence of the observers inwardly experiencing all that is going on? In view of their presence and their attitudes toward Catholic moral teaching, we now are confronted with the question: what is the hope for the future in this area?

Perhaps it will be helpful to cite another statement of Cullmann's:

What separates us—apart from divergent concepts of unity—are not the positive component elements of our faith. It is rather that Catholicism has *more* (for our part we would say: it has in excess) and conversely that we have *less* (from the Catholic standpoint it would be: lack of something on our side). In my opinion the dialogue will make progress when our Catholic brethren cease to consider as simply and purely negative this *less* which they find on our side. This means that they would not look upon it as lack and arbitrary restriction but as a conscious concentration on that which according to our opinion must remain the sole center of our faith in Christ. For this very reason we welcome at the Council every proposal for renewal of liturgical life and theological endeavor which is directed toward such concentration and deplore every further development of the *more* in the sense indicated above.

In moral theology the response to this concern might be: Christ is the indispensable center of the moral message of the Church, also in our presentation of moral theology, and precisely in the presentation of moral theology which presumes to be scientific. Would it not perchance be better if our presentation in certain instances renounced its claim to the *more* (which some find an excess) rather than gave up the clear and appreciative proclamation of the whole Christ, crucified and risen from the dead?

But there is a *more* which we cannot renounce if we are to have a more conscious concentration inspired by the Holy Spirit. And indeed we have no need at all to renounce it for the sake of the ecumenical dialogue, nor will it at all offend as more or excess if it receives its full meaning from the one Center.

An example may help clear up this point. Our tracts of moral theology on the natural right and the natural moral law appear to many of the separated brethren as hazardous excess. To my mind only a more profound presentation of our best Catholic tradition with a stress on that doctrine according to the Bible would be necessary. In the actual economy of salvation there is no natural moral law without supernatural roots. According to the thought of the Prologue of the Gospel of John and the Epistle to the Colossians, everything must be viewed in the light of Christ, consciously beginning with Him, awaiting His triumph. "He is the image of the invisible God, the firstborn of every creature. For in him were created all things in the heavens and on the earth, things visible and things invisible, whether Thrones, or Dominations, or Principalities, or Powers. All things have been created through and unto him, and he is before all creatures, and in him all things hold together" (Col 1,15-17).

A consciously Christocentric exposition of the doctrine on natural law, or more specifically on the revealed plan and order of creation, involving a more dynamic view of salvation history from the plenitude of Catholic tradition— above all from biblical thought—this is just as possible or even more possible and more coherent than an anthropocentric, nonhistoric, and static view which unfortunately has been in considerable vogue among Catholics. Such a concentration on salvation history would have no reason to sacrifice a single element of truth. Perhaps indeed it might free us from a baneful more insofar as concentration and emphasis and the degree of certainty of utterance are concerned. It is sufficient to study the history of the doctrine on natural law even within the Catholic Church to discover with what fatal ease a purely static and nonhistorical approach to the actual realities of a certain age and culture made them appear part and parcel of eternal principles.

Conscious concentration on the entire moral of the mystery of the Word incarnate should appeal to the separated brethren. At the same time such a concept would necessarily eliminate one of their objections to our moral doctrine—what they consider an incomprehensible excess: the juridical and canonical casuistry in our manuals of doctrine and in our moral instruction. Actually this has done violence to the balanced harmony of our moral teaching which is present in the Gospel and was apparent in the classical tradition down to the time of St. Bernard and St. Thomas.

The simplification of canon law as such was explicitly planned by John XXIII from the very day of the proclamation of the Council. Above all, an effort will be made to enunciate clearly the perspectives of the Christian life. Ecclesiastical law and sound obedience to it can be of profit— not by any extension of the law, but only through a more profound and purer penetration of it—if the "law of Christ," the "law of the Spirit of the life in Christ Jesus," animates everything and places all things in proper balance.

The Eastern Church and the noblest representatives of Protestant Christianity, beginning in the spirit of our current moral theology with the goal and purpose of the commandment for the perfect love of God, consider the Christian life more dynamically as a continuous conversion. The better Catholic tradition, including the Council of Trent,[1] tends in the same direction. But a truly open dialogue with genuine Catholic generosity between Catholics and separated brethren should help us to discover our own heritage and make it more fully our own.

Our own moral directed to the sacrament of penance— moral conceived onesidedly for the office of judge, and concerned with the confessor and the obligation of integral confession on the part of the Christian—has also a more. It consists in the precise demarcation between mortal sins and venial sins, simply incomprehensible to the separated brethren of the Orient and the Occident. Here also a sincere dialogue with others demands basically more reflection on our own heritage. We can see that things were not always as they were in the past century, nor do they always have to remain that way. The limitations and restrictions of law as applied from below must be balanced in right measure with the glad tidings of Christian love, with the directive from above.

In its better representatives, Protestant theology looks upon the expression of the balance between the glad tidings and the moral obligations in the sequence *Gospel and law* rather than *law and the Gospel*, as a matter of great importance. And we Catholics can and must revert to our origins, to our most ancient heritage. Gratefully we must draw from these pure wells of doctrine and present our

[1] See Session 14, Denz. (32) 1694.

moral theology as the glad tidings, as the paschal exultation. In this way the encounter with our separated brethren will be rendered easy.

A loving approach to the Christian life in the atmosphere of the resurrection in union with our separated brethren of the East should preserve us from the typical Western tendency to deal with our religious life on the level of ideas and concepts. By contrast with that of the East, which is most intimately concrete, our instruction and our moral pedagogy are dominated by this hypernotionalistic and conceptualistic approach. The devout of the Eastern rites turn above all to the visible manifestation of the eternal love of the Father in the person, in the figure of Christ, in His example, in His saints. The images of Christ and the saints derive their signification from the fact that the saints themselves all together are imitations of Christ. And Christ Himself is the perfect image of the Father and the primal pattern of our life. We latecomers of the West looked upon our images and statues as the Bible of the poor. We thought that we could largely give up the indicative signs (the comprehensible images) in our celebration of the liturgy, to say nothing of our marked preference for the overemphasis of a dead sacral language. The more seriously we desire the return of the communities of the Eastern Church to the one Church of Christ, seeking to this end to comprehend their own proper conception of the moral message, the more readily will we arrive at that authentic Catholic concentration on our abundant spiritual riches, which the Evangelical Christians will love as much as do the Christians of the Eastern rites.

The separated brethren will no longer have reason to take umbrage at a few instances of what they consider as excessive and irrelevent to a great center if within the Catholic breadth and fullness they perceive more distinctly our Catholic center.

On the occasion of a congress of the home missions, one of the men present thought he could blithely dismiss an allusion to the pastoral experiences in France with the observation, "In pastoral matters we Germans have nothing to learn from the French." The entire group reacted violently: "Above all, we have to learn that we can learn from everybody."

In this period of the Council, this hour of grace, we are so happy in our faith that we acknowledge with gratitude that we can learn also from our separated brethren. We are happy above all when an inexorable love impels them to inquire regarding the complete picture of Catholicity. If they have helped us arrive at a better understanding of our common heritage in our paternal house, have we not learned much from them?

Therefore, the forces at work for some thirty years for the renewal and deepening of Catholic moral theology truly owe much to the biblical, liturgical, and patristic renewal. The work already begun will surely be able to reach a stage of greater fruitfulness if in all things we are motivated by an ardent desire for the fulfillment of the will of the Lord, "that they all may be one."

ADDRESS OF JOHN XXIII AT THE OPENING
OF THE SECOND VATICAN COUNCIL[1]

Venerable brothers, Mother Church rejoices today in the singular generosity of divine providence: the longed-for day has dawned on which the Second Vatican Ecumenical Council opens solemnly, here at the tomb of St. Peter. It is placed under the patronage of the Virgin Mother of God, whose maternal dignity we celebrate in today's feast.

Ecumenical Councils in the Church

All councils, the twenty ecumenical and the countless others, provincial or regional—whose importance should not be underestimated—plainly reveal the vigor of the Catholic Church through the course of the ages, for like stars in a brilliant sky they brighten the pages of her history.

In convoking this vast assembly, the present humble successor of the Prince of the Apostles who now addresses you planned to reaffirm the teaching office of the Church,

[1] [AAS, November 26, 1962, pp. 786 ff. The above translation and the summaries are taken directly from this official version.—Tr.]

which continues unbroken to the end of time. By means of this Council here assembled the teaching office should study the errors, the needs, the opportunities of our time. And in its work it should be proclaimed in an extraordinary manner to all men throughout the whole world.

Wherefore, in opening this universal synod, the Vicar of Christ now addressing you turns to the ages of the past. Naturally we must hearken to the voice from the past. It is alert and full of life, confirming our minds. Eagerly we recall the great merits of the sovereign pontiffs of the distant past and of more recent times who have transmitted through the ages the testimony of this same earnest and venerable voice. It has re-echoed from the councils held in the Orient and in the Occident from the fourth century to the Middle Ages and down to our own times, attesting with ceaseless effort to the triumph of that divine and human Society, the Church of Christ, who derives from the divine Redeemer her title, her gifts of grace, and all her vitality.

[In the next paragraph the Pope refers to the trials and sorrows which have afflicted the Church and clouded her history for nineteen centuries. From the beginning men were aligned with Christ or turned against Him. Herein lies the problem which the Pontiff next takes up.]

In fact, the tremendous problems and difficulties which mankind must face have not changed in nearly two thousand years, for Christ Jesus is the eternal Center of life and history: men either cling to him and His Church—and in consequence enjoy the blessing of life, tranquillity, right order, and peace—or they live apart from Him, attack Him, and deliberately remain aloof from His Church. The result is internal disorder, bitterness in human relations, and the threat of bloody wars.

Wherever they assemble, ecumenical councils solemnly proclaim this union between Christ and His Church. They also diffuse the light of truth everywhere. They guide men in the way of virtue in individual, domestic, and social life. They arouse and strengthen spiritual energies and continually raise the minds of men to blessings which are true and eternal.

[In the four subsequent paragraphs the Pope refers to the evidence of this "extraordinary magisterium of the Church, namely, of the universal councils" found in the archives of Rome and in libraries throughout the world. The thought of the Council came to him almost as a divine inspiration. There were three years of work in preparation, which are like a "sign and gift of heavenly grace." The Pontiff is confident of the outcome.]

Illuminated by the light of this Council, the Church, we fondly hope, will be spiritually enriched. She will draw from it a renewal of her energies and intrepidly face the future. In fact, through the introduction of opportune changes and a system of mutual cooperation intelligently organized, she will succeed in turning the minds of individuals, families, peoples to the things which are above.

[The Council suggests that we thank God and celebrate the glory of Christ. The very circumstances are propitious. Our age is not the worst of all ages, as though "in the period of the preceding councils all things were ideal regarding Christian doctrine, morals, the Church's rightful liberty." The Pope turns to the future with optimism.]

We should rather say that in the present course of events which places the family of mankind on the threshold of a new order of things we must acknowledge the inscrutable designs of divine providence. As the ages roll by these hidden designs attain their purpose through human efforts. But often they transcend the expectations of men, for God wisely disposes all things, even human misfortune, to the good of the Church.

[So concerned are men today with critical economic and political problems, the Pontiff adds, that they pay but slight heed to the spiritual concerns of the Church. Though we cannot approve of such an attitude, it does bring about some good: current conditions have at least removed many obstacles which formerly stood in the way of the Church's freedom. In some instances rulers in a sincere attempt at exercising patronage over the Church harmed the cause of religion through political and selfish procedures. Though he rejoices that the Church is now finally freed from many secular encumbrances of past ages, the Pope is saddened by the absence from the Council of prelates who are imprisoned for the faith in Christ or otherwise deprived of their freedom. "Now from this Vatican Basilica as from a second apostolic cenacle" the Church "can earnestly raise her voice with all its majesty."]

The Principal Task of the Council: To Safeguard and Teach the Divine Truth

The greatest concern of the Council is to safeguard and explain the sacred heritage of Christian teaching more effectively.

[This doctrine embraces the whole man and directs him to eternity. It shows how we are to fulfill our duties as citizens of earth and heaven and thus attain the goal for which God destines us. Men must strive for this goal as individuals and as members of society through the right use of earthly things. We must first seek the kingdom of God, but not to the neglect of duties of the terrestrial order. Works of love performed in the spirit of evangelical perfection contribute mightily to the strength and growth of human society.]

But in order that this teaching influence the various spheres of human activity—in private, domestic, and social life—it is essential first of all that the Church keep her eyes fixed on that sacred heritage of truth handed down from the Fathers. At the same time it is essential that she look to the present, to the new conditions and new forms of life which have opened up new avenues to the Catholic apostolate in the world today.

[The Church has not been indifferent to the marvelous progress in science and invention. Nor has she failed to assess their value. She has directed men to look beyond this earth, even when they subject the earth to their dominion, and to turn to the Source of all wisdom and beauty, to God Whom we must adore.]

The Present-Day Method of Explaining the Church's Doctrine

From what we have just said, the role the Council is expected to play in the teaching of doctrine is quite apparent.

This twenty-first Ecumenical Council purposes to present in all its integrity and without diminution or distortion the Catholic doctrine which despite difficulties and controversies has become the common heritage of mankind. To this end it will avail itself of the effective assistance of experts in all branches of sacred science, in the apostolate and in administration. This expert assistance is of paramount importance and is highly esteemed in the Church. Even though the doctrine is not welcomed by all, it is offered to all men of good will as a treasure of inestimable value and available to all.

Our duty is not only to guard this treasure as though we were concerned with antiquity alone; we must further be alert and fearless in dedicating ourselves to the task which the present age imposes upon us. We must pursue a course which the Church has followed for nearly twenty centuries.

The principal objective which our task envisions is not to discuss certain primary areas of ecclesiastical doctrine in order to restate the traditional teaching of the Fathers and the theologians of former days and of more recent times in greater detail. We have good reason to assume that this teaching has long been known and cherished by you. Hence, there is surely no need to convoke a council merely to organize discussions of this kind.

What is needed at the present time is that the whole Christian doctrine in its integrity be universally accepted with renewed zeal and with peaceful and tranquil minds, and without any distortion of that accuracy in conception and that precise form of presentation in words which are especially evident in the acts of the Councils of Trent and First Vatican. What is required and what all sincere lovers of the Christian Catholic apostolic ideal ardently crave is that this same doctrine be more widly known and more deeply understood and that men's spirits be more fully imbued with it and formed in it. It is essential that this doctrine, certain and immutable, to which we owe dutiful acceptance, be studied and explained in accordance with the needs of our own age. The deposit of faith itself or the truth which is contained in our time-honored teaching is one thing; the manner in which it is set forth, in full integrity of sense and meaning, is another. Indeed, much consideration must be devoted to this manner of presentation, and if need be a painstaking effort must be made to elaborate it. This is to say that ways and means of exposition must be sought which are more in harmony with the magisterium whose character is predominantly pastoral.

How Errors Are To Be Suppressed

[The Lord's truth is eternal. Human ideologies change, and human errors often vanish as quickly as they arise.]

At no time did the Church fail to oppose these errors. She often acted with unyielding firmness and condemned them. But in this present age the Spouse of Christ prefers to apply the balm of mercy rather than take up the arms of severity and punishment. She is convinced that present-day needs are more wisely served by explaining the value of her doctrine more fully than by condemning the errors which contradict it. This is not to say that we do not encounter hazards and false doctrines and opinions today. There is no lack of them. We must guard against them and dispel them. However, they are all so obviously at variance with what is basically right and just and have produced such deadly fruit that men today spontaneously are inclined to condemn them. In this connection those forms of life which ignore God and His laws, place excessive confidence in technical progress, and center well-being exclusively in the comforts of life are to be particularly noted. It is becoming increasingly evident that the dignity of the human person and true self-realization are subjects of great moment and most difficult to achieve. But what is even more important, men have finally learned by experience that violence imposed on other men, armed might, and political dominion are totally inadequate to provide a happy solution to the extremely knotty problems which beset them.

Under these circumstances, the Catholic Church as she raises aloft the torch of religious truth through this Ecumenical Council seeks to show herself the loving mother of all men, kindly, patient, and filled with mercy and goodness toward the children separated from her. To the human race, oppressed by so many difficulties, she says what Peter once said to the wretched man who begged an alms of him: "Silver and gold I have none; but what I have, that I give thee. In the name of Jesus Christ of Nazareth, arise and walk" [Acts 3,6]. The Church does not offer to the men of our time corruptible wealth. She does not promise mere earthly bliss; but she does bestow on them the gifts of supernatural grace, which since they elevate men to the dignity of sons of God, are genuine defense and assistance in making their life more fully human. She opens the fountains of her life-giving doctrine so that illumined by the light of Christ, men may fully understand what they really are, how exalted is their dignity, what goals they must seek. Through her children she enlarges the frontiers of Christian love everywhere, for nothing is so effective in eradicating the seeds of discord and promoting harmony, peace, justice, and universal brotherhood.

Unity To Be Fostered in the Family of Christians and in the Family of Mankind

Great indeed is the desire of the Church to promote and safeguard the truth in accordance with the design of God, "who wishes all men to be saved and to come to the knowledge of the truth" [I Tm 2,4]. Her desire arises from her conviction that men are not capable of arriving at the absolute and unshakable unity of minds which is bound up with genuine peace and eternal salvation without the support of the whole body of revealed truth.

Sad to relate, however, the entire Christian family has not yet attained full and perfect visible unity in truth. But the Catholic Church considers it her duty to strive earnestly for the fulfillment of the great mystery of that unity for which Christ Jesus prayed so ardently to His heavenly Father on the eve of His sacrifice. The realization that she is connected so intimately with this prayer of Christ creates ineffable sweetness of peace and joy in the Church. Should she not rejoice sincerely when she sees this prayer produce the most abundant and salutary fruits even among those who are outside her fold? Indeed, if we consider the matter rightly, this very unity which Jesus Christ besought for His Church seems to glow with a threefold ray of salutary supernal light. We have a corresponding threefold unity: the unity of Catholics among themselves, which must always be most firm and exemplary; the unity of devout prayer and most ardent desire prompting the Christians separated from this Apostolic See to aspire to be united with us; and finally, the unity based on esteem and respect for the Catholic Church shown by those who profess diverse forms of religion though they have not reached the point [non adhuc] of becoming Christians.

It is sad indeed, in the light of all this, that an immense portion of the human race—even though no one is born on this earth who is not also redeemed by the blood of Christ —does not share the sources of supernatural grace which are in the Catholic Church. Hence the Catholic Church, whose light shines upon all, whose force of supernatural unity redounds to the benefit of the entire family of men, is aptly described by the following magnificent passage of St. Cyprian:

The Church, radiant with the light of her Lord, sheds her rays over the entire world. Though it radiates everywhere, the light is still one; and the unity of her body is unbroken. She extends her fruitful branches over the whole earth; she sends out her flowing streams over an ever expanding domain; but the Head is one. The source is one. She is the one Mother bringing forth children, generation after generation: she gives us birth, she nourishes us with her milk, she animates us with her spirit.[2]

Venerable brethren, such is the goal of the Second Vatican Synod. It summons the Church's best energies to united effort, earnestly striving to have men welcome the tidings of salvation ever more generously. In this way it prepares and protects the course leading to that unity of the human race which is necessary as a foundation for the construction of the terrestrial city in the pattern of the heavenly city, whose king is truth, whose law is love, whose measure is eternity.[3]

Conclusion

Truly, venerable brethren in the episcopate, "our heart is wide open to you" [II Cor 6,11]. Look about you. We are

[2] St. Cyprian, De Cath. Eccl. Unitate, 5.
[3] St. Augustine, Epist. 138, 3.

gathered here in this Vatican Basilica, where the decisive events and turning points of the Church's history center, where at this very moment heaven and earth are united in the most intimate of bonds. We are in the very shadow of St. Peter's tomb and the tombs of so many sainted predecessors of ours, whose ashes seem now to thrill in mystical exaltation.

As the Council opens, a new day dawns in the Church, a day resplendent in radiant light. It is only the dawn and already the first rays of the rising sun have gently set our hearts aglow! Here all things breathe the spirit of holy joy. For around us enhancing the grandeur of this temple by their splendor are the stars, which according to the testimony of John the Apostle you are; and in your persons, as golden candelabra shining around the tomb of the Prince of the Apostles the churches which you represent are present [Ap 1,20]. With you we see the men of great dignity who have come to Rome from the five continents of the earth. In a spirit of deep humility and fervent expectation, they are present in the name and person of their nations.

It would not be false to say that the citizens of heaven and earth are cooperating in the celebration of the Council. The blessed have their role—to watch over and protect us in our work; the faithful have their role—to pray ardently to God; you have your role—to respond obediently and promptly to the supernatural impulses of the Holy Spirit and to do all in your power to make your efforts correspond to the needs and expectations of all nations. To achieve this you will need minds serene in their possession of peace, the spirit of brotherly harmony, moderation in your approach, dignity in discussion, and wisdom in all your deliberations.

May your zeal and your work abundantly fulfill these expectations. Not only are the eyes of all mankind upon you, but also all the world's hopes.

[The address closes with the prayer for divine assistance.]